**Video Workbook 2** | **Units 30 to 58**

Written by Katherine and Steve Bilsborough, Jo Cummins,
Barbara Mackay, Teresa Payman, Susannah Reed

## Contents

| | | | |
|---|---|---|---|
| Unit 30 | Where is Ziggy? ................... 2 | Unit 44 | Animals all around ................ 44 |
| Unit 31 | Where's Mr Clarke? ............... 5 | Unit 45 | My mobile phone ................. 47 |
| Unit 32 | Your classroom ..................... 8 | Unit 46 | Hurry up! Time to go! ........... 50 |
| Unit 33 | On the farm ........................ 11 | Unit 47 | Books are cool! ................... 53 |
| Unit 34 | It can fly! ............................ 14 | Unit 48 | There's a monster ............... 56 |
| Unit 35 | Photos of my family ............ 17 | Unit 49 | Hobbies ............................ 59 |
| Unit 36 | We love fashion! ................. 20 | Unit 50 | We like playing sports ......... 62 |
| Unit 37 | At the restaurant ................ 23 | Unit 51 | It's the weekend ................. 65 |
| Unit 38 | Time for lunch .................... 26 | Unit 52 | Time to do your chores ....... 68 |
| Unit 39 | Where are my friends? ........ 29 | Unit 53 | What does she do everyday? ... 71 |
| Unit 40 | The big red bus .................. 32 | Unit 54 | My dad's daily routine ......... 74 |
| Unit 41 | Let's make a smoothie ........ 35 | Unit 55 | On the beach ..................... 77 |
| Unit 42 | Welcome to my shop ........... 38 | Unit 56 | The sea is nice and blue ...... 80 |
| Unit 43 | Looking at the animals ........ 41 | Unit 57 | On my street ...................... 83 |
| | | Unit 58 | They are sitting in the sun ... 86 |

© ELT Songs Ltd 2021
First published in 2021 by ELT Songs Ltd

All rights reserved. No part of this publication may be reproduced, stored in a retrieval system, communicated or transmitted in any form or by any means without prior written permission. All inquiries should be made to ELT Songs Ltd.

Text design by Andrew Magee
Cover design by Andrew Magee
Edited by Sarah Bennetto

Illustrations by Flora Aranyi / Beehive Illustration Agency
Photographs used under license from Shutterstock.com

ISBN
Print: 978-1-7399494-2-6

**Nova Stars Unit 30** Song

# Where is Ziggy?

**1** Watch the music video 🎵 and tick ✏️.

**2** Find 🔍 and circle 5 differences ✏️

**Fast finishers** Draw your bedroom with some of your toys.

**How do you feel? Colour.**

# Nova Stars Unit 30 — Vocabulary

**1** Read 📖 and match ✏️. Say 💬. [5]

bath   bed   rug
cupboard   toy box   desk

**2** Look 🔍 and write ✏️. [5]

1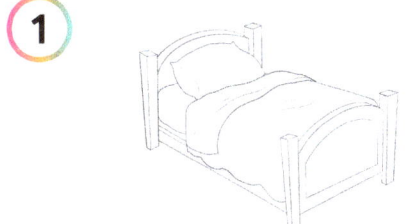
b e d

2
_ _ _ _

3
_ _ _ _

4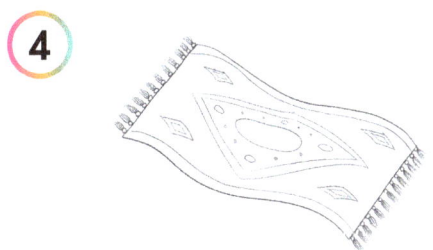
_ _ _

5
_ _ _   _ _ _

6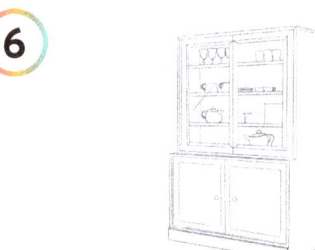
_ _ _ _ _ _ _ _

**Fast finishers** What's in your bedroom? Find and colour.

**How do you feel? Colour.**

# Nova Stars Unit 30 — Grammar

## 1 Look, read and tick ✓ or cross ✗. | 4

1 Dad is in the toy box. ✓
2 The book is under the rug.
3 My hat is in the cupboard.
4 Ziggy is on the desk.
5 The cat is under the desk.

## 2 Look and write. | 3

Where's Ziggy?
_He's in_ the cupboard.

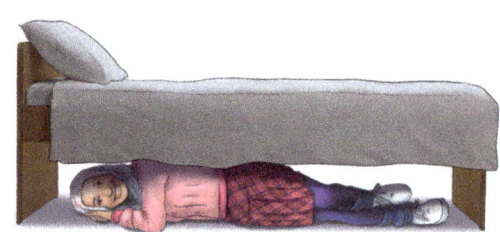

Where's Kim?
She's _____ the bed.

Where's my book?
_____ the rug.

Where's Alex?
_____

**Fast finishers** Work with a friend. Put a pencil in different places. Ask and answer *Where's the pencil?*

How do you feel? Colour.

# Where's Mr Clarke?

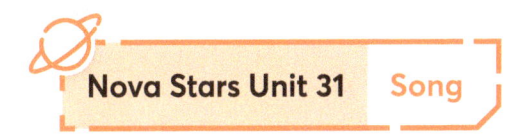

**1** Watch the music video 🎵. Look and tick ✓ or cross ✗ .

**2** Look 🔍 and match ✏️.

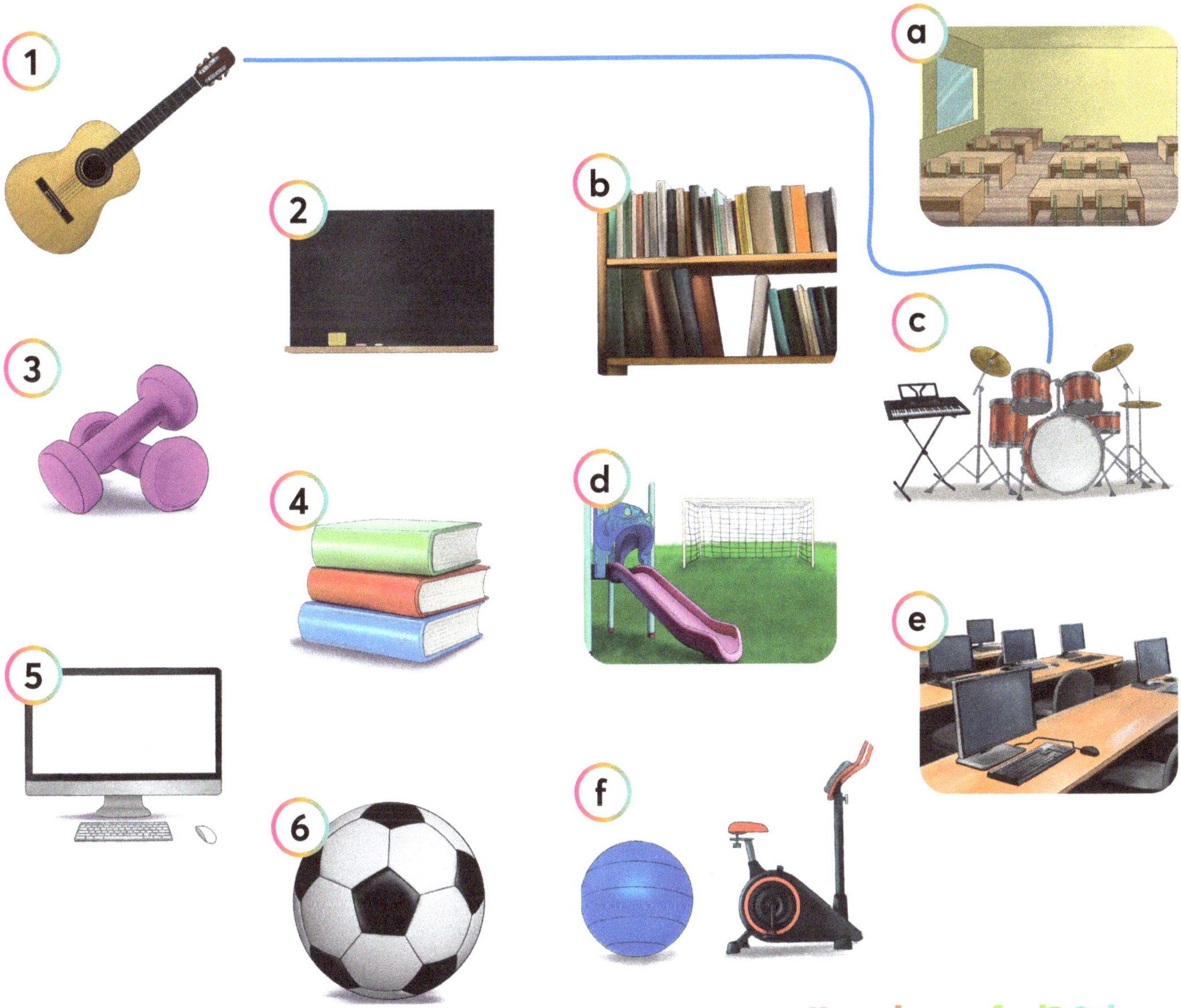

**Fast finishers** Draw your favourite place at school.

**How do you feel? Colour.**

**Nova Stars Unit 31** | Vocabulary

### 1. Read 📖 and circle ✏️. Say 💬. [3]

1. (library) / computer room

2. music room / computer room

3. playground / gym

4. classroom / music room

### 2. Look 🔍 and write ✏️. [5]

1.

4.

5.

3.

6.

¹c l a s s r o o m

**Fast finishers** Mime some places at school for your friend to say.

**How do you feel? Colour.**

He**'s** in the classroom.
→ He **is** in the classroom.

**Nova Stars Unit 31 — Grammar**

## 1 Look and circle. 3

**1**  Where's Ziggy?
He **is** / **isn't** in the gym.

**2**  Where's Grace?
She **is** / **isn't** in the classroom.

**3**  Where's Alex?
He **is** / **isn't** in the library.

**4**  Where's David?
He **is** / **isn't** in the music room.

## 2 Read and write. 4

**Where's** Miss White?

She isn't ✗ in the library.

_____ Alice?

She _____ ✓ in the music room.

_____ Tom?

_____ ✗ in the computer room.

**Fast finishers** Write questions and answers about where people are in your school.

**How do you feel? Colour.**

**Nova Stars Unit 32** Song

# Your classroom

**1** Watch the music video 🎵. What do you see? Tick ✓.

1 ✓

2

3

4

5

6

**2** Look 🔍 and draw ✏️

 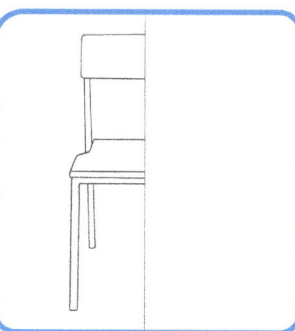 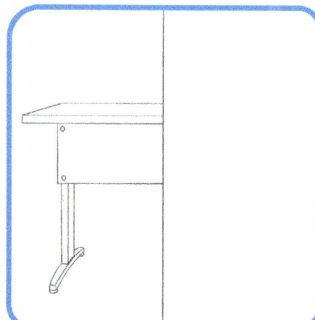 

  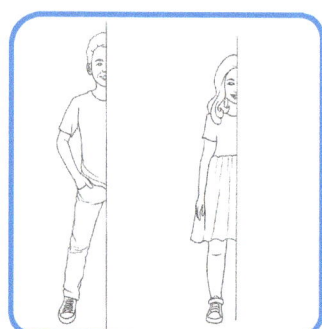 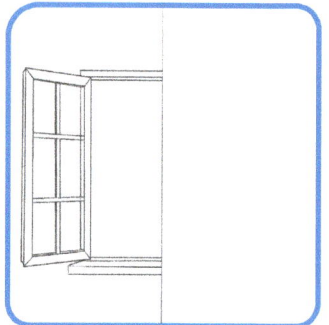

**Fast finishers** Draw your classroom.

**How do you feel? Colour.**

**Nova Stars Unit 32** Vocabulary

**1** Look and match. Say. 5

1 ch — ld
2 po — cher
3 chi — air
4 bo — dow
5 tea — ard
6 win — ster

**2** Look, write and match. 3

clock  posters  chairs  ~~teacher~~

1 There's a _teacher_ in the library.

2 There are ................ on the wall.

3 There are ................ in the classroom.

4 There's a ................ in the computer room.

**Fast finishers** Point and say what you see in your classroom.

**How do you feel? Colour.**

## Nova Stars Unit 32 — Grammar

**1  Look and circle.** [3]

1 Is there a clock?
  (Yes, there is.)    No, there isn't.
2 Are there any chairs?
  Yes, there are.    No, there aren't.
3 Is there a window?
  Yes, there is.    No, there isn't.
4 Are there any books?
  Yes, there are.    No, there aren't.

**2  Complete the questions with *Is there* or *Are there*. Look and write the answers.** [5]

1  <u>Are there</u> any posters in the classroom?
   <u>Yes, there are.</u>

2  <u>Is there</u> a desk in the gym?
   _____

3  _____ a chair in the library?
   _____

4  _____ any children in the playground?
   _____

**Fast finishers** What's in your classroom? Ask and answer questions using *Is there…?* or *Are there…?*

How do you feel? Colour.

# On the farm

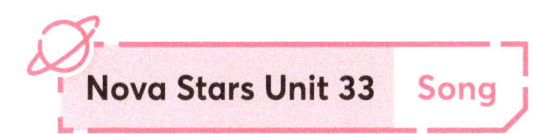

**1** Watch the music video 🎵. Which animals are on the farm? Tick ✔ or cross ✖.

**2** Look, count and write.

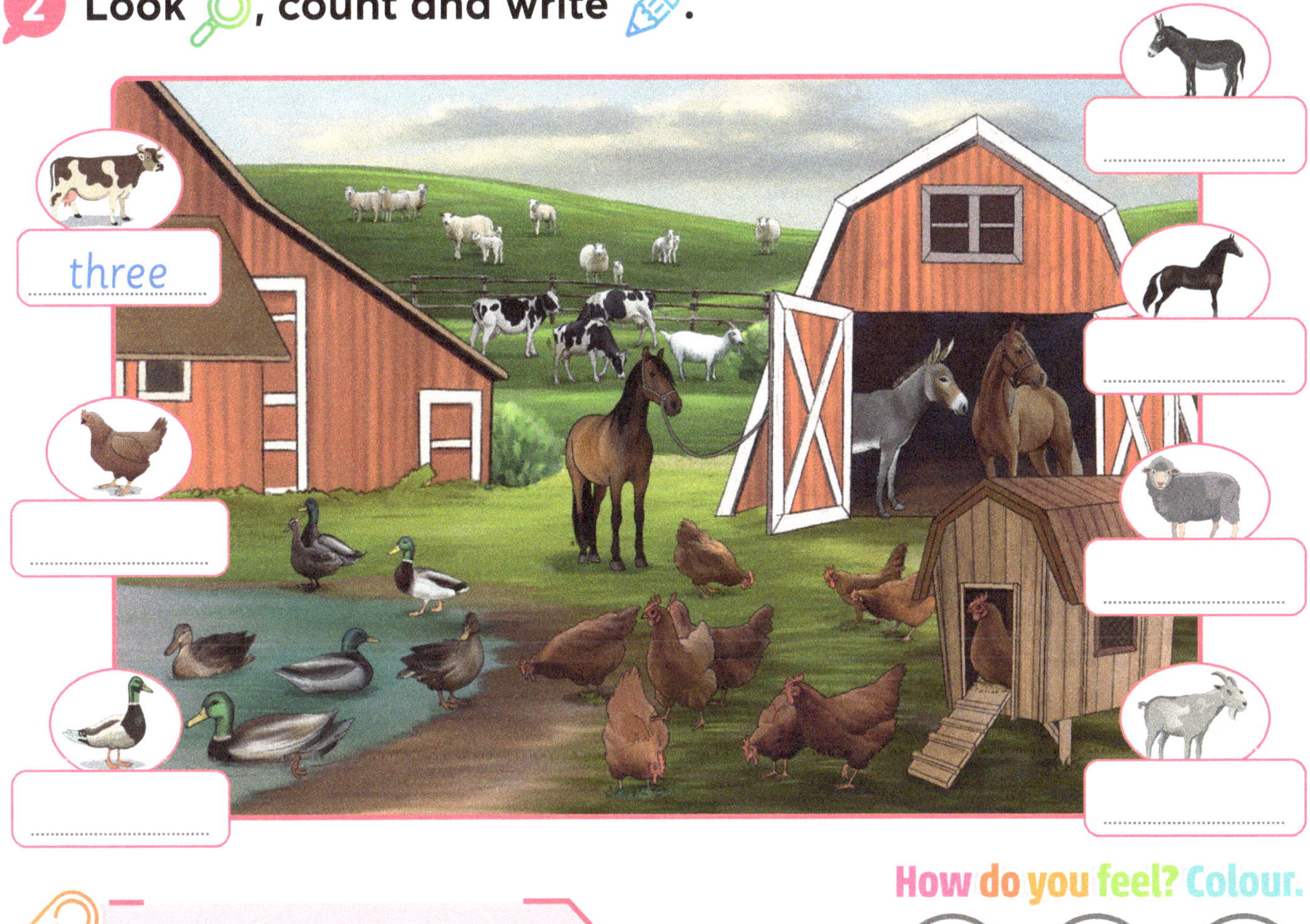

Fast finishers Draw a cat and a dog on the farm.

**How do you feel? Colour.**

**Nova Stars Unit 33** | **Vocabulary**

**1** Read and match. Say. | 4

goat

cow

sheep

donkey

chicken

**2** Look and write. | 5

cow

**Fast finishers** Colour your favourite animal in activity 2.

How do you feel? Colour.

Nova Stars Unit 33 | Grammar

## 1 Look, read and tick ✓. 3

**1** Can you see the dog?

Yes, I can. ✓
No, I can't. ☐

**2** Can you see the chicken?

Yes, I can. ☐
No, I can't. ☐

**3** Can you see the cat?

Yes, I can. ☐
No, I can't. ☐

**4** Can you see the goat?

Yes, I can. ☐
No, I can't. ☐

## 2 Look, read and write. 5

**1.** Can you see the cows?
*Yes, I can.*

**2.** Can you see the chicken?
...................................

**3.** Can you see the dog?
...................................

**4.** Can you see the goats?
...................................

**5.** Can you see the cat?
...................................

**6.** Can you see the horse?
...................................

**Fast finishers** Look around you. What can you see? Ask a friend.

**How do you feel? Colour.**

**Nova Stars Unit 34** — Song

**It can fly!**

**1** Watch the music video 🎵. Colour the animals you see ✏️.

1   2   3

4   5   6

**2** Look 🔍 and write ✏️.

1   2   4 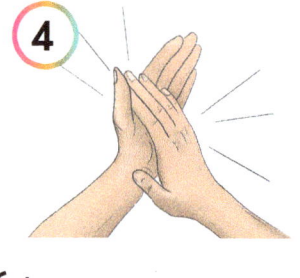  5

3   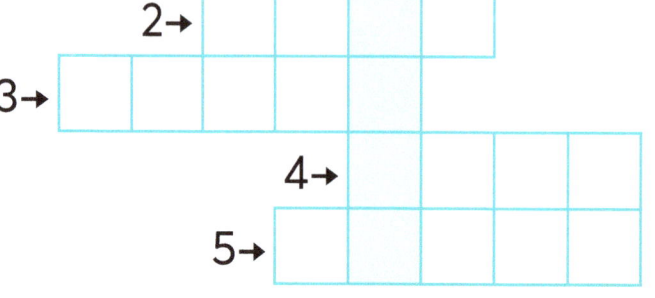  6

1→ c o u n t

**Fast finishers** Mime the actions for a friend.

**How do you feel? Colour.**

### 1. Read 📖 and circle ✏️. Say 💬.  [ 4 ]

 swim  
(jump)

 run  
talk

 jump  
fly

 run  
talk

 fly  
swim

### 2. Look 🔍 and write ✏️.   run   ~~swim~~   jump   talk   fly   [ 4 ]

1. **swim**
2. ........................
3. ........................
4. ........................
5. ........................

**Fast finishers** Circle the animals in the picture that can fly.

**How do you feel? Colour.**

**Nova Stars Unit 34**  Grammar

### 1 Look, read and match. [ 3 ]

a  b  c  d

**1** It can swim.   **2** It can't fly.   **3** It can fly.   **4** It can't swim.
It can jump.        It can run.          It can't sing.       It can fly.
It can't fly.       It can't talk.       It can't run.        It can sing.

### 2 Look and write. [ 9 ]   draw  fly  jump  run  swim  talk

1  It can ___run___.
   It can't ___draw___.
   It can't _____.

2  It can ___talk___.
   It can't _____.
   It can't _____.

3  _____.
   _____.
   _____.

4  _____.
   _____.
   _____.

**Fast finishers** What can you do? Write.

**How do you feel? Colour.**

# Photos of my family

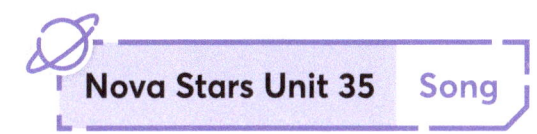 Nova Stars Unit 35 — Song

**1** Watch the music video 🎵. Tick ✓ the people in Alex's family ✏️.

**2** Find 🔍 and circle 5 differences ✏️.

**Fast finishers** Find and circle the animals in activity 2. Say.

**How do you feel? Colour.**

Nova Stars Unit 35 Song  17

**Nova Stars Unit 35** Vocabulary

1 **Read and match. Say.** | 4

mum  father  auntie  grandpa  grandmother

dad  aunt  grandfather  grandma  mother

2 **Write the words on the family tree.** | 5

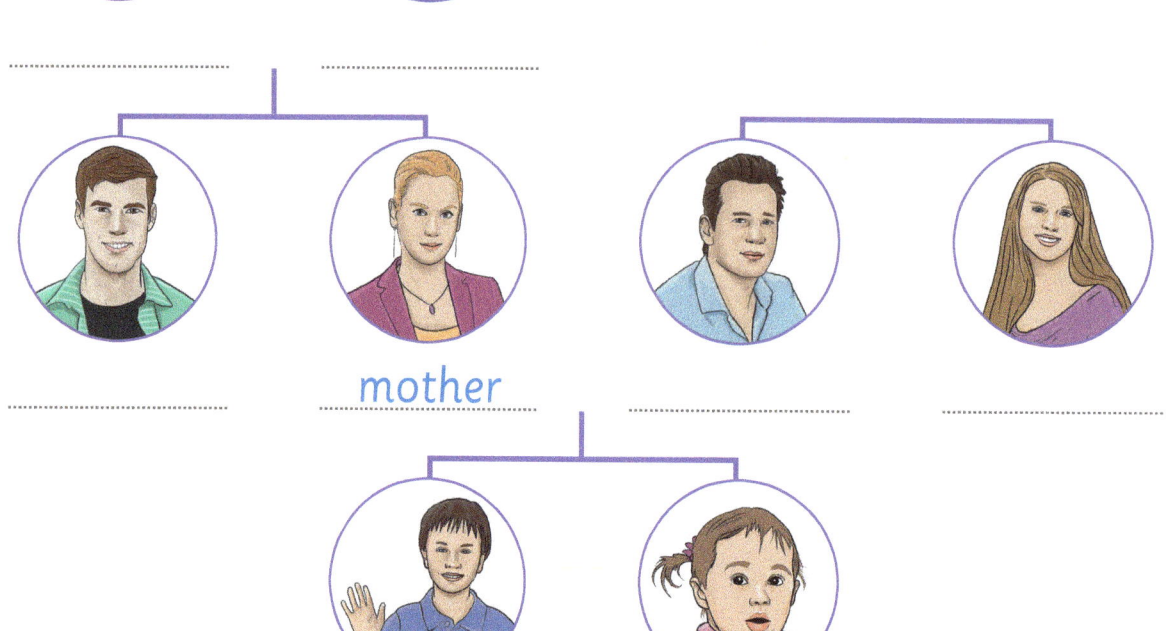

~~mother~~  uncle  grandmother
father  aunt  grandfather

mother

me     sister

**Fast finishers** Draw your family tree.

How do you feel? Colour.

Nova Stars Unit 35 Grammar

1 Read  and write . 5

A: Is she your mother?

B: No, she isn't. My mother has got short hair. She's my aunt. She's got long hair.

A: Is he your father?

B: Yes, he is. He's got glasses.

A: Is he your grandfather?

B: No, he isn't. He's my uncle. He's got black hair. My grandfather is old. He's got white hair.

2 Read  and write . 3

1
Aunt Lily

Is she your mother?

No, she isn't.

2
Grandfather

Is he your grandfather?

3
Father

Is he your uncle?

4
Mother

Is she your mother?

 **Fast finishers** Draw people in your family. Ask and answer with a friend.

How do you feel? Colour.

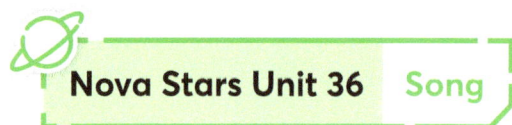

**Nova Stars Unit 36** Song

# We love fashion!

**1** Watch the music video 🎵 and match ✏️.

**2** Find 🔍 and circle 6 differences ✏️. Say 💬.

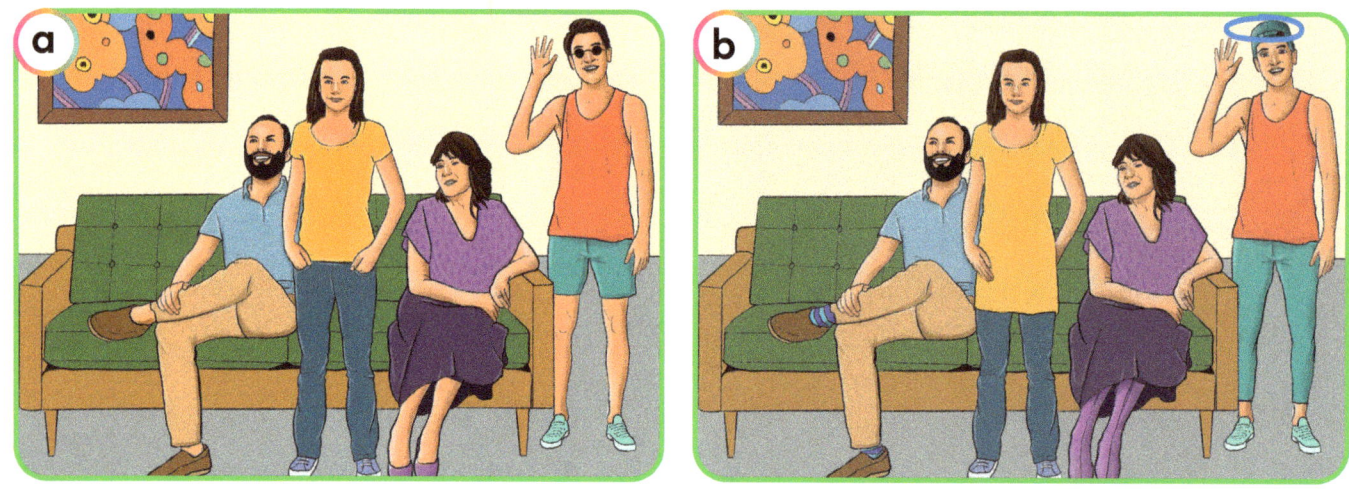

**Fast finishers** Draw and colour a T-shirt for your favourite Planet Popstar.

**How do you feel? Colour.**

Nova Stars Unit 36 Vocabulary

**1** Look and write the clothes. Colour the pictures. | 5

1. 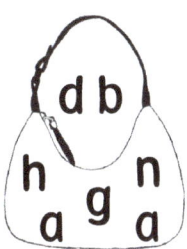 h a n d b a g

2.  _ _ _ _ _

3. 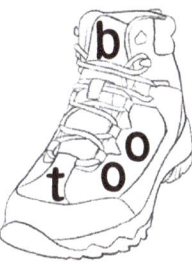 _ _ _ _

4.  _ _ _ _

5.  _ _ _ _ _ _

6.  _ _ _ _ _

**2** Look and write. | 3

1.
What's this? It's a boot.

2.
What are these? They're _____.

3.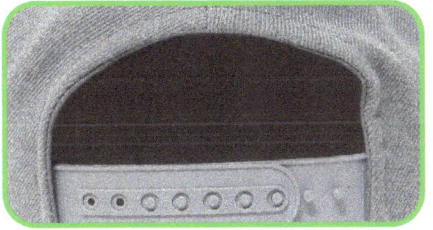
What's this? It's a _____.

4.
What are these? They're _____.

**Fast finishers** Write two sentences about your clothes today. Use *I'm wearing …*

How do you feel? Colour.

**Nova Stars Unit 36** Grammar

**1** Read, look and write the letter. | 3 |

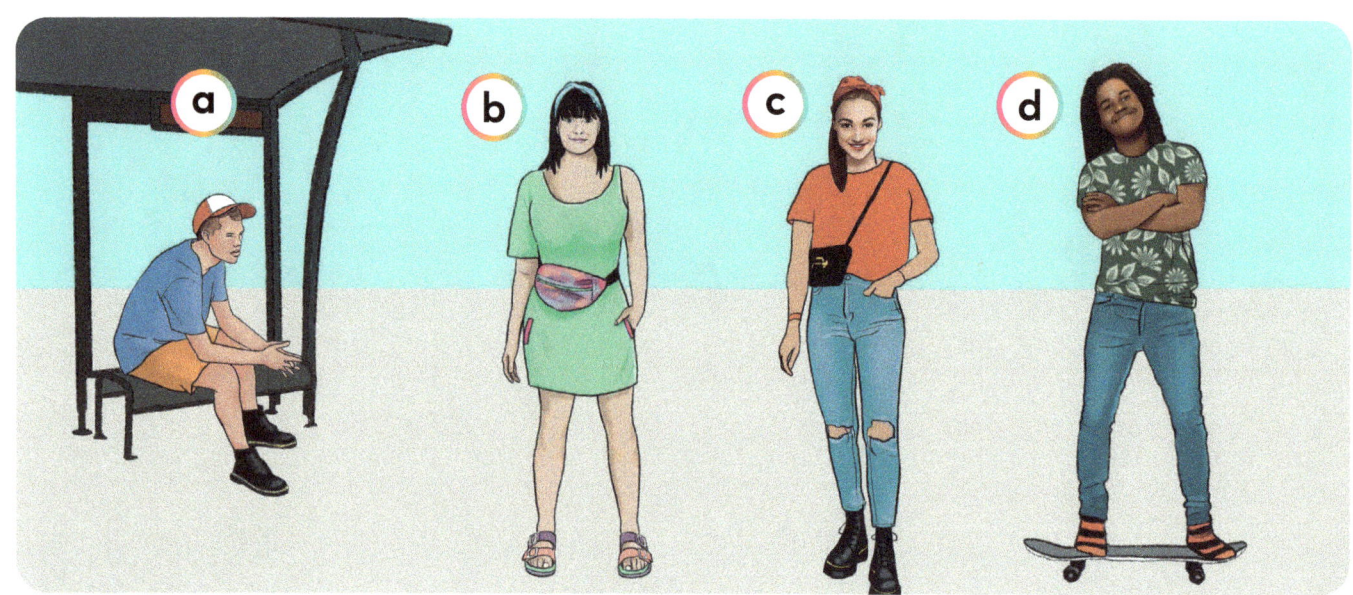

1 She's wearing boots. **c**      3 He's wearing a baseball cap. ......
2 She's wearing a dress. ......      4 He's wearing jeans. ......

**2** Look and write. | 4 |

<u>She's wearing</u> a baseball cap.

She's ............... a skirt.

She ............... a handbag.

............... socks.

............... .

**Fast finishers** With a friend, talk about different people in your classroom. Say *He's / She's wearing …*

**How do you feel? Colour.**

# At the restaurant

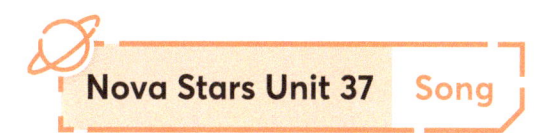

**1** Watch the music video 🎵 and tick ✓ the food you see ✏️.

**2** Look 🔍 and match. Which food is missing? Circle ✏️.

**Fast finishers** Circle the food you like in activity 1.

**How do you feel? Colour.**

# Nova Stars Unit 37 Vocabulary

## 1 Look and write. | 5

burger   chips   meatballs   ~~noodles~~   pasta   rice

1 ..................
2 ..................
3 ..................
4 ..................
5 ..................
6 noodles

## 2 What's next? Circle and say. | 4

1        (rice) / noodles

2       burger / chips

3        noodles / pasta

4        burger / meatballs

5        chips / pasta / rice

**Fast finishers** Draw a burger and colour it.

How do you feel? Colour.

Nova Stars Unit 37 — Grammar

**1** Number the sentences. Practise with a friend. | 4 |

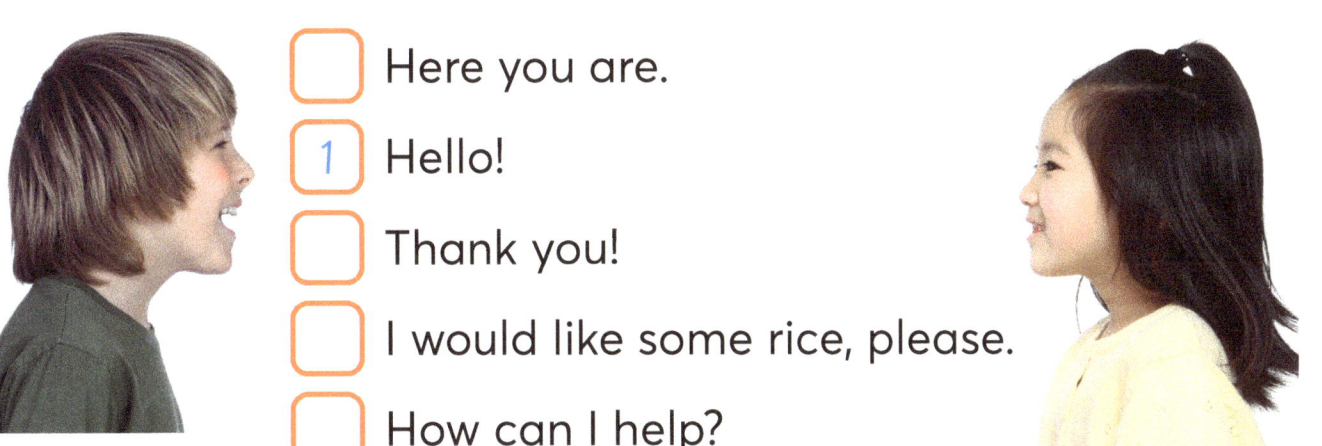

- [ ] Here you are.
- [1] Hello!
- [ ] Thank you!
- [ ] I would like some rice, please.
- [ ] How can I help?

**2** Look and write. | 5 |

1  *I would like* meatballs and _____.
2  I would like _____ and a _____.
3  _____ pasta and _____.

**Fast finishers** Write a conversation in a café. Use the words from this lesson.

How do you feel? Colour.

**Nova Stars Unit 38** Song

# Time for lunch

**1** Watch the music video 🎵. Colour the food in the song ✏️.

| 1 | 2 | 3 | 4 | 5 |
|---|---|---|---|---|
|  | 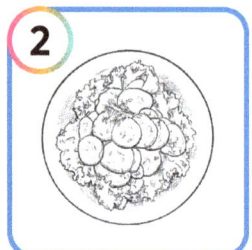 |  |  |  |
| 6 | 7 | 8 | 9 | 10 |
| 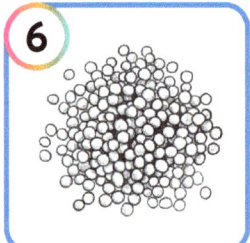 |  |  |  |  |

**2** Look , read and match .

> I've got chicken for my lunch.
> I haven't got chips or salad.
> I've got potatoes and tomatoes.
> I've got some juice to drink.

a

b

c

d

**Fast finishers** Make a list of the food words you know.

**How do you feel? Colour.**

**1** Read 📖 and draw ✏️. Say 💬. | 4 |

1
salad

2
carrots

3
peas

4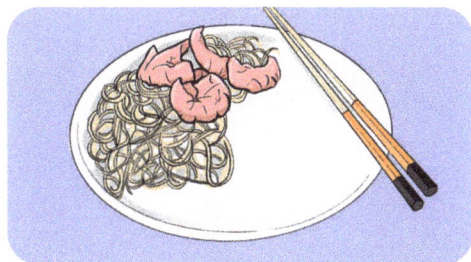
beans

**2** Look 🔍 and write ✏️. | 5 |

beans ~~carrots~~ onions
peas potatoes salad

1  I would like _carrots_ and _____, please.

2  I would like _____ and _____, please.

3  I would like _____ and _____, please.

**Fast finishers** Write a list of five green foods. Then draw.

How do you feel? Colour.

# Nova Stars Unit 38 — Grammar

## 1 Read, match and write. [3]

**Yes, please.    No, thanks.**

1 Would you like potatoes?
2 Would you like carrots?
3 Would you like beans?
4 Would you like onions?

a ..........................
b ..........................
c ..........................
d Yes, please.

## 2 Look and write. [4]

Would you like peas and ..........................

Yes, ..........................

.......................... ?

No, ..........................

**Fast finishers** Ask your friend what food they want. Say *Would you like …?*

**How do you feel? Colour.**

# Where are my friends?

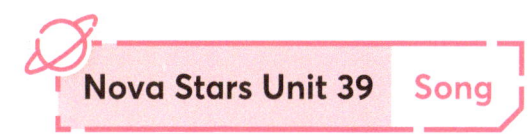 **Nova Stars Unit 39** Song

**1** Watch the music video 🎵 and number ✏️.

 a
 b
 c
 d — 1

 e
 f
 g
 h

**2** Find 🔍 and colour the matching place ✏️.

 1

 2
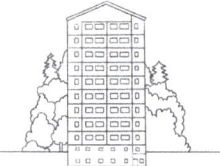

 3

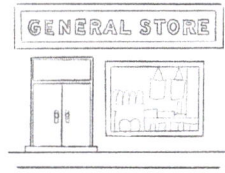

 4

🚀 **Fast finishers** Find, circle and colour Ziggy.

**How do you feel? Colour.**

# Nova Stars Unit 39 — Vocabulary

**1** Read and match. Say. 6

playground · café · flat · house

park · bookshop · shop

**2** Follow and write. 4

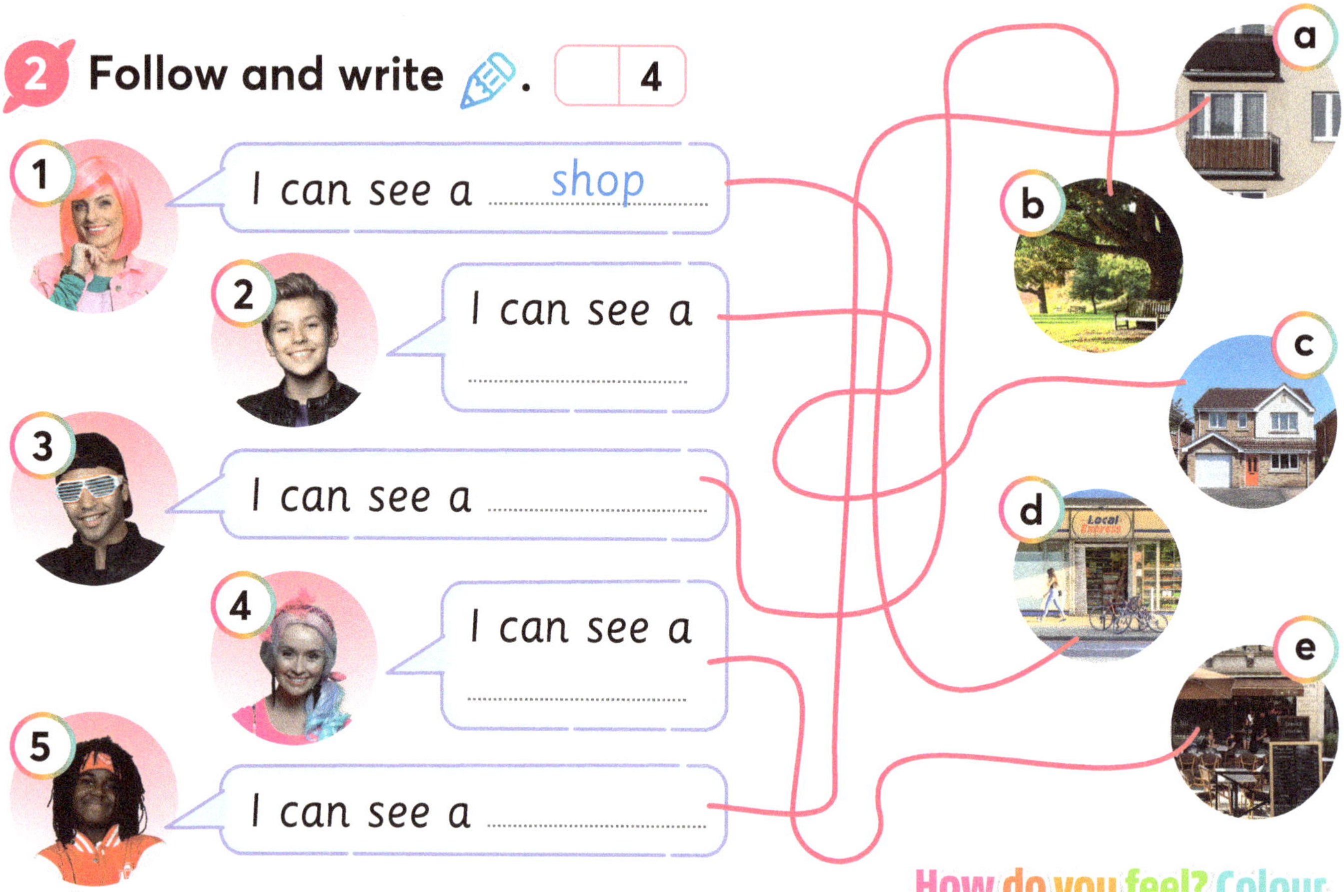

1. I can see a _shop_
2. I can see a ..........
3. I can see a ..........
4. I can see a ..........
5. I can see a ..........

**Fast finishers** What can you see from your classroom window? Think and say.

How do you feel? Colour.

**Nova Stars Unit 39** Grammar

### 1 Read and tick. 3

**1** Where are they?

They aren't at the park.
They're at the playground.

**2** Where are they?

They aren't at the café.
They're at the bookshop.

**3** Where are they?

They aren't at the shop.
They're at the house.

**4** Where are they?

They aren't at the flat.
They're at the library.

### 2 Look and write sentences. 2

bookshop   café   ~~flat~~

Where are Alice and Hugo?

*They aren't at the flat.*

**Fast finishers** Play a game. Mime where Alice and Hugo are now. Your friend says *They aren't at … They're at…*

**How do you feel? Colour.**

# The big red bus

**1** Watch the music video 🎵. How does Sarah go to school? Look and tick ✓ or cross ✗ ✏️.

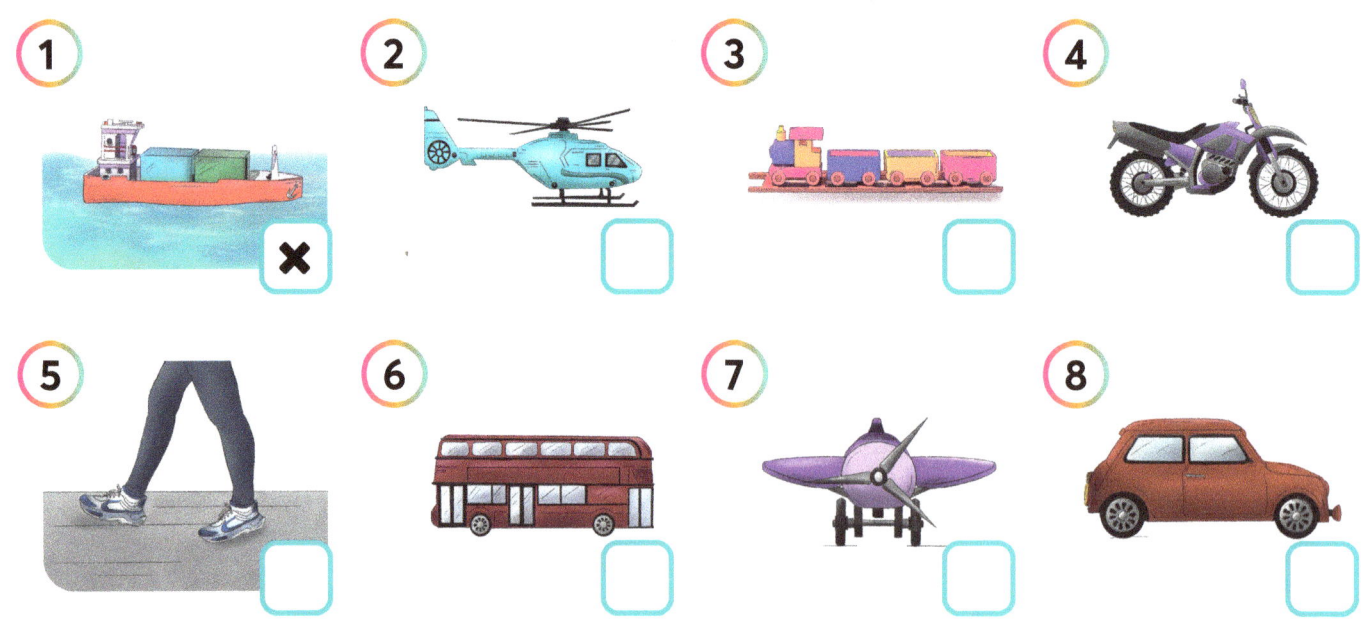

**2** Find 🔍 and circle 6 differences ✏️.

**Fast finishers** Draw a picture of a big red bus. Draw your friends in the windows.

How do you feel? Colour.

Nova Stars Unit 40 Vocabulary

**1** Find 🔍, colour and match ✏️. Say 💬.  | 5

- boat
- bus
- car
- helicopter
- motorbike
- train

**2** Look and write ✏️. Say 💬.  | 3

1. Let's go by _train_
2. Let's go on _____
3. Let's go by _____
4. Let's go by _____

**Fast finishers** Mime a type of transport. Your friend says *Let's go by …*

**How do you feel? Colour.**

# Nova Stars Unit 40 — Grammar

**1** Look and follow. Read and write. [3]

1. I go to school by bike. — May
2. I go to the park by car. ....................
3. I go to the playground on foot. ....................
4. I don't go to the library by train. ....................

**2** Read and write about you. [6]

I go to .................... on foot. I don't go .....................
I .................... by car. I don't ......................
....................

**Fast finishers** How do you go to school? Draw a picture and write: *I go to school ….*

How do you feel? Colour.

# Let's make a smoothie

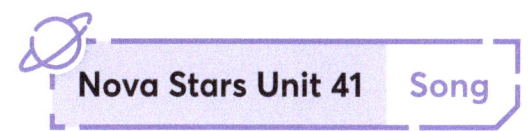

**1** Watch the music video 🎵. Which fruit is missing? Draw ✏️.

**2** Find 🔍 and colour the fruit ✏️.

**Fast finishers** Write a list of all the fruit you know. Then circle your favourites.

**How do you feel? Colour.**

**Nova Stars Unit 41** Vocabulary

**1** Read and circle. Say. | 5

1. smoothie / (pineapple)
2. coconut / pineapple
3. mango / lime
4. mango / kiwi
5. lime / mango
6. smoothie / lemon

**2** Look and write. | 5

| 1 | c | o | c | o | n | u | t |
| 2 |   |   | m |   |   |   |   |
| 3 |   | i |   |   |   |   |   |
| 4 |   |   |   | i |   |   |   |
| 5 |   | a |   |   |   |   |   |
| 6 |   |   |   |   | p |   |   |   |

**Fast finishers** Write a list of fruit to make your favourite smoothie.

How do you feel? Colour.

**Nova Stars Unit 41** Grammar

**1** Look and tick ✔ or cross ✘. | 4

1. We've got a few kiwis. ............
2. We haven't got any pineapples. ............
3. We've got a lot of apples. ............
4. We haven't got any grapes. ............

any  few  four
got  lemons  lots
~~limes~~  many

**2** Look, read and write. | 7

1. How many _limes_ have we got? — We've got ............ limes.
2. How ............ bananas have we got? — We've got a ............ bananas.
3. How many pineapples have we ............? — We've got ............ of pineapples.
4. How many ............ have we got? — We haven't got ............ lemons.

**Fast finishers** Tell a friend what fruit you have and haven't got at home.

**How do you feel? Colour.**

**Nova Stars Unit 42** Song

**Welcome to my shop**

**1** Watch the music video 🎵. Tick the object that is NOT in the song ✏️.

**2** Watch again. Tick ✔ what you can touch and cross ✖ what you can't touch ✏️.

1  ✖

2

3

4

5

**Fast finishers** Draw a technology shop with your favourite things in the shop window.

**How do you feel? Colour.**

# Nova Stars Unit 42 — Vocabulary

## 1 Look. Write and match. 5

1 p c m o u t r e — computer
2 a m c r a e — ..........
3 e m o s u — ..........
4 b t l a t e — ..........
5 y k b e o a d r — ..........
6 o d r i a — ..........

a. (camera)
b. (tablet)
c. (keyboard)
d. (computer)
e. (radio)
f. (mouse)

## 2 Look and write. 5

Don't touch the radio !

Don't touch .......... !

Don't .......... !

.......... !

.......... !

.......... !

**Fast finishers** Write three sentences with 'Don't touch' about technology in your classroom.

**How do you feel? Colour.**

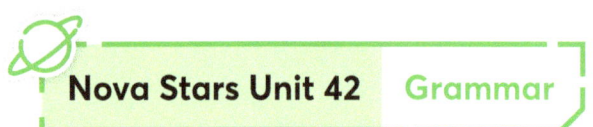

## Grammar

**1** Look, read and write. | 3

1 ✗  d
2 ✓
3 ✓
4 ✗

a — Can I use the radio? / No, you can't, sorry.

b — Can I use the tablet? / Yes, of course.

c — Can I use the radio? / Yes, of course.

d — Can I use the tablet? / No, you can't, sorry.

**2** Look and write. | 3

1 Can I use the computer?

2 ................................................?

3 ................................................?

4 ................................................?

**Fast finishers** Practise asking and answering questions with *Can I use …?*

**How do you feel? Colour.**

# Looking at the animals

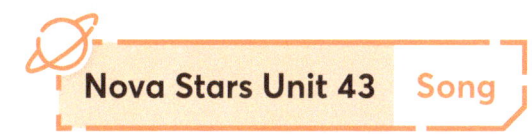

Nova Stars Unit 43 | Song

**1** Watch the music video 🎵. Tick the animals in the song ✏️.

**2** Find 🔍 and circle 5 differences ✏️.

**Fast finishers** Which animals in the pictures can swim? Circle and count.

**How do you feel? Colour.**

# Nova Stars Unit 43 — Vocabulary

**1** Look and find more words. Make another word with the extra letters. | 5

a e l e p h a n t n m o n k e y i b e a r m h i p p o a t i g e r l

1 elephant
2 ...........
3 ...........
4 ...........
5 ...........
6 a _ _ _ _ _

**2** Look and write the names of the animals. | 4

1 elephants     2 ...........     3 ........... 
4 ...........   5 ...........

**Fast finishers** Make a list of all the animals you know. Show your lists to each other.

How do you feel? Colour.

**1** Read and tick. | 3 |

1 I'm looking at the monkeys.
   I'm not looking at the monkeys. ✓

2 I'm looking at the bears.
   I'm not looking at the bears.

3 I'm looking at the hippos.
   I'm not looking at the hippos.

4 I'm looking at the snakes.
   I'm not looking at the snakes.

**2** Look and write sentences. | 4 |

1 ✓ 🐘 I'm looking at the elephants.

2 ✗ 🦛 I'm not looking at the bears.

3 ✗ 🦓 ......

4 ✓ 🐱 ......

5 ✗ 🐝 ......

6 ✓ 🌸 ......

**How do you feel? Colour.**

**Fast finishers** Write two true sentences with *I'm looking at … I'm not looking at …*

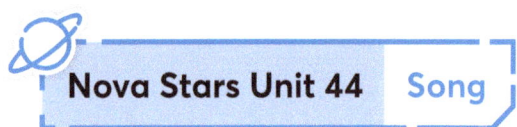

# Animals all around

**1** Watch the music video 🎵 and number ✏️.

**2** Circle the odd-one-out ✏️.

1.

2.

3.

4.

**Fast finishers** Draw and colour your favourite animal.

**How do you feel? Colour.**

**Nova Stars Unit 44** — Vocabulary

**1** Look and match. Say. | 5

1 play
2 sleep
3 drink
4 rest
5 eat
6 climb

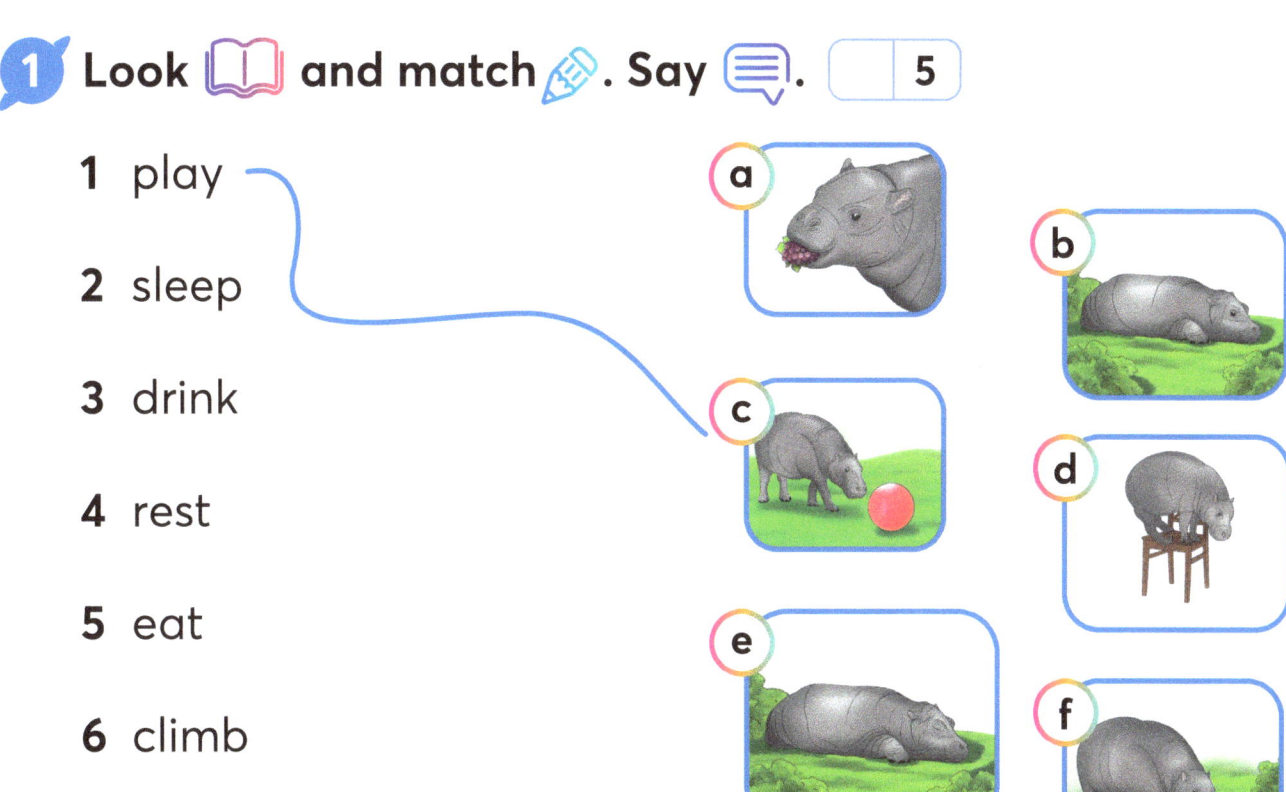

**2** Look and write. | 5

1 sleep
2
3
4
5
6

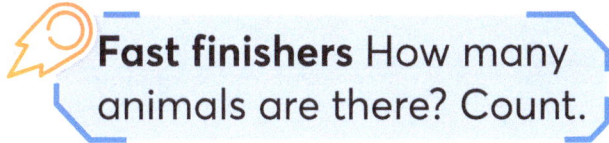
**Fast finishers** How many animals are there? Count.

**How do you feel? Colour.**

# Nova Stars Unit 44 Grammar

## 1 Read and circle. 4

1 It's sleeping.

2 It isn't eating.

3 It isn't drinking.

4 It's playing.

5 It's resting. 

## 2 Look and write. 6

climbing   drinking   eating   ~~playing~~   sleeping

1 _It isn't_ eating.
   _It's playing_.

2 .................... playing.
   ....................

3 .................... resting.
   ....................

4 ....................
   ....................

**Fast finishers** Point at the animals on this page and say. _It isn't (playing). It's (sleeping)._

**How do you feel? Colour.**

# My mobile phone

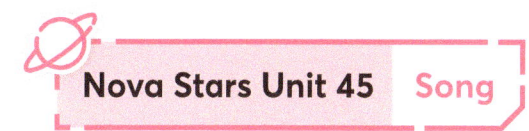 **Nova Stars Unit 45** — Song

**1** Watch the music video 🎵. What do you see? Tick ✓ or cross ✗ ✏️.

1. ✓ 
2. ☐ 
3. ☐ 
4. ☐ 
5. ☐ 
6. ☐

**2** Look 🔍 and match ✏️

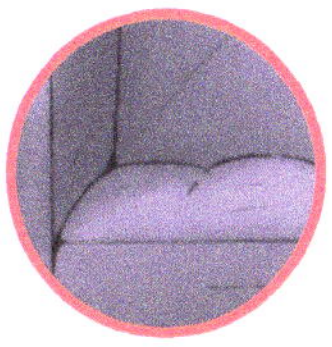

**Fast finishers** Find and circle the animals in the picture. Say.

**How do you feel? Colour.**

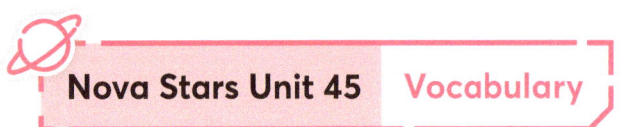 Nova Stars Unit 45  Vocabulary

**1** Read and circle. Say.  5

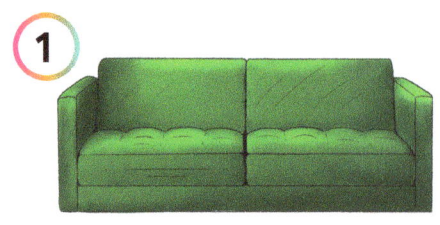  

(sofa)  door       armchair  wall       table  sofa

table  bookcase       bookcase  door       armchair  wall

**2** Look and write. 5

| | | ¹t | ²a | b | l | e |
| | | | | | | |

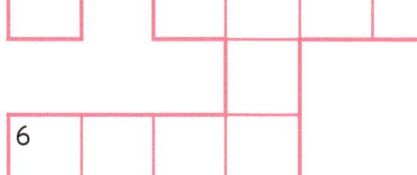

**Fast finishers** Find the furniture in your classroom. What colour is it?

How do you feel? Colour.

Nova Stars Unit 45 Grammar

**1** Read and circle. 4

1 **(They're)** / **They aren't** on the wall.

2 **It isn't** / **It is** under the table.

3 **They're** / **They aren't** behind the armchair.

4 **They're** / **They aren't** on the bookcase.

5 **It is** / **It isn't** in front of the sofa.

**2** Look. Write sentences with the words in (brackets). 3

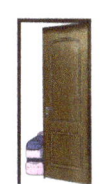
1 <u>It's behind the door.</u> (it / behind)

2 _____ the armchair. (they / in front of)

3 _____ the sofa. (it / behind)

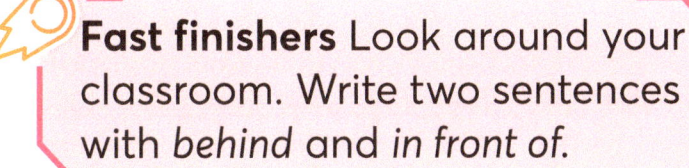
4 _____ the cupboard. (they / in front of)

**Fast finishers** Look around your classroom. Write two sentences with *behind* and *in front of*.

**How do you feel? Colour.**

# Nova Stars Unit 46 Song

## Hurry up! Time to go!

**1** Watch the music video 🎵 and tick the popstars you see ✏️.

**2** Look 🔍 and match ✏️.

**Fast finishers** Colour the pictures in activity 2.

**How do you feel? Colour.**

**Nova Stars Unit 46** Vocabulary

**1** Read and match. Say. 5

1 TV
2 mirror
3 lamp
4 mat
5 plant
6 painting

a
b
c
d
e
f

**2** Find and write. 5

 1

TV

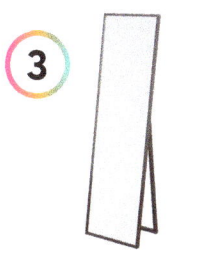 3

 5

| d | g | n | r | l | h | a | z |
| p | a | i | n | t | i | n | g |
| u | m | k | l | v | o | f | m |
| e | p | l | a | n | t | p | i |
| m | j | v | p | q | r | y | r |
| a | a | s | b | a | c | i | r |
| t | k | l | a | m | p | x | o |
| s | T | V | o | v | w | m | r |

2

4

6

**Fast finishers** Spell the words with a friend.

**How do you feel? Colour.**

## Starters Unit 46 Grammar

### 1 Read  and circle . | 3

1 Is it next to the TV?
Yes, it is.
(No, it isn't.)

2 Are they between the chair and the table?
Yes, they are.
No, they aren't.

3 Is it in front of the bookcase?
Yes, it is.
No, it isn't.

4 Are they under the table?
Yes, they are.
No, they aren't.

### 2 Look  and write . | 4

1 Where are the chairs? _Are they_ under the window? _Yes, they are_.

2 Where's the sofa? _____ it between the armchair and the lamp? _____, it _____ .

3 Where are the paintings? _____ next to the window? _____ .

**Fast finishers** Ask and answer questions about the picture in activity 2.

**How do you feel? Colour.**

# Books are cool!

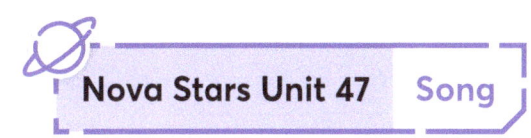

**1** Watch the music video 🎵. Look 🔍 and circle the books you see. ✏️

**2** Look 🔍 and match ✏️.

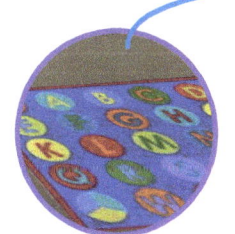     

**Fast finishers** Can you find the cat in activity 2?

**How do you feel? Colour.**

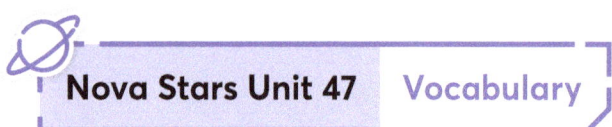

# Nova Stars Unit 47 — Vocabulary

**1** Read 📖 and match ✏️. Say 💬.  4

funny   scary   fantasy   adventure   fairy tale

**2** Follow and write the Planet Popstars' favourite books ✏️.  4

fairy tales   ~~adventure~~   fantasy   funny   scary

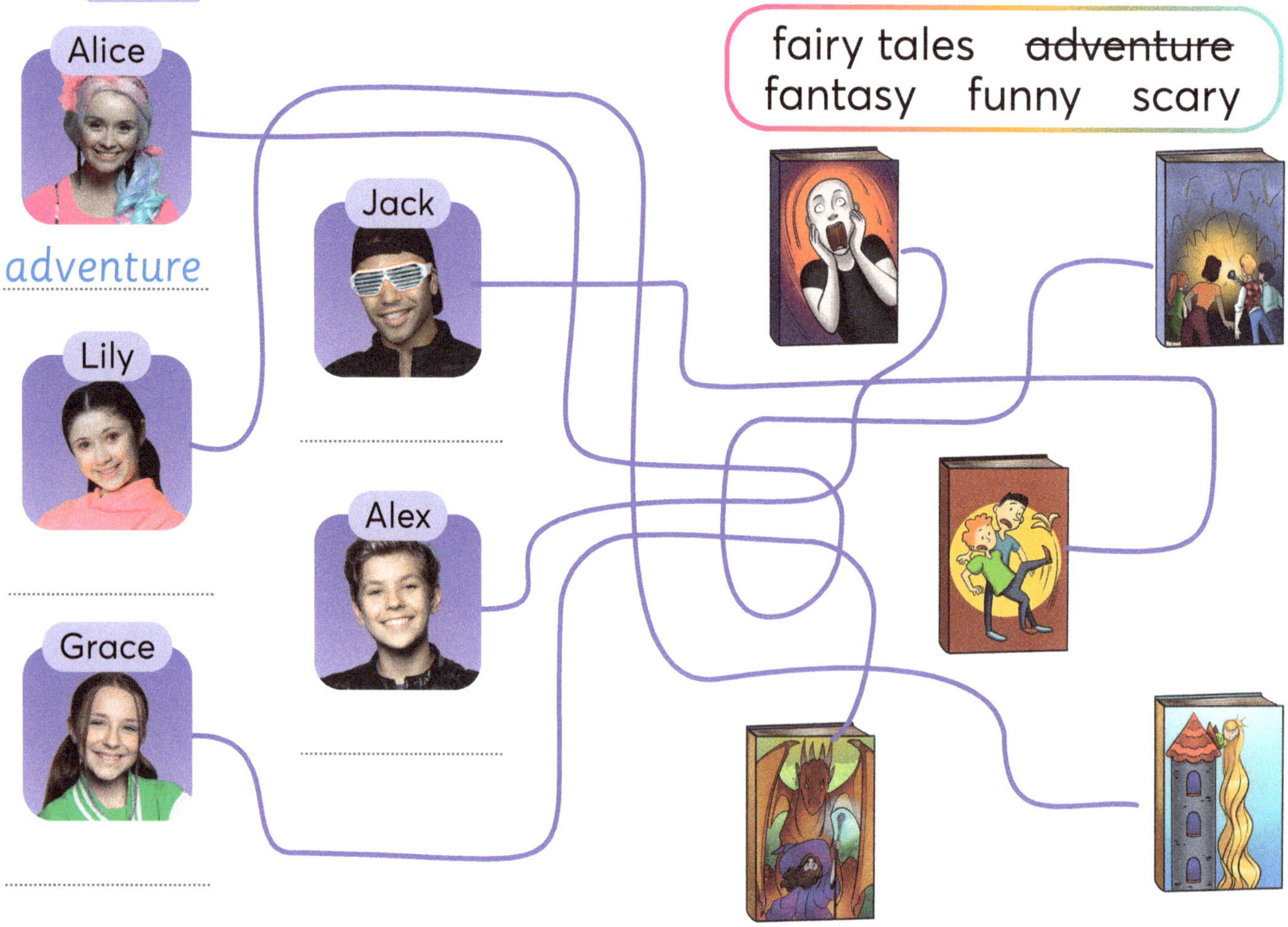

Alice — adventure

Lily — ...........

Jack — ...........

Alex — ...........

Grace — ...........

**Fast finishers** What books do you like? Write a sentence.

How do you feel? Colour.

Nova Stars Unit 47 | Grammar

**1** Look  and write . | 4

Yes, he / she does.    No, he / she doesn't.

1  Does she like fantasy books?
..................

2  Does he like funny books?
..................

3  Does she like adventure books?
..................

4  Does he like fairy tale books?
..................

**2** Write the words in order. Answer the questions . | 7

**1** your friend / like / books / fantasy/ Does ?

*Does your friend like fantasy books?*

**2** like / Does / books / your friend / adventure ?

..................

**3** Does / fairy tale / your friend / like / books ?

..................

**4** scary / books / like / your friend / Does ?

..................

 **Fast finishers** With a new partner, ask and answer the questions about your friends.

How do you feel? Colour.

**Nova Stars Unit 48** Song

There's a monster

**1** Watch the music video 🎵. Match ✏️.

**2** Look 🔍. Circle the two pictures that are the same ✏️.

**Fast finishers** Which types of books can you remember? Write a list.

How do you feel? Colour.

Nova Stars Unit 48 Vocabulary

# 1 Read and tick ✔ or cross ✘. [5]

 1 This is a wizard! ✔

 2 This is a girl!

 3 This is a princess!

 4 This is a monster!

 5 This is a boy!

 6 This is a prince!

# 2 Look and write. Say. [6]

princess  boy  ~~witch~~  wizard  girl  prince  monster

1 witch
2 ..........
3 ..........
4 ..........
5 ..........
6 ..........
7 ..........

**Fast finishers** Draw a scary monster. Write sentences about your monster *It's / It isn't (big). It's got (six heads).*

**How do you feel? Colour.**

**Nova Stars Unit 48** Grammar

**1** Read  and match . 3

a) My favourite book is about a dog and a wizard. The dog is very small. It's an adventure book.

b) My favourite book is about a witch. She has a small house and a pet cat. The cat can talk!

c) My favourite book is about a prince and a princess. They have a white horse. The horse can fly!

d) My favourite book is about a very small monster. He wants to be scary. His dad is very big and he's got four eyes!

**2** Read  and write . 5

What's your favourite book?

My favourite book is _____

What's it about?

It's about _____

Has it got a monster? _____

Has it got a witch? _____

Is it funny? _____

**Fast finishers** Ask a friend about his / her favourite book.

How do you feel? Colour.

# Hobbies

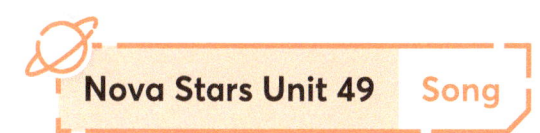 **Nova Stars Unit 49** Song

**1** Watch the music video 🎵 and number ✏️.

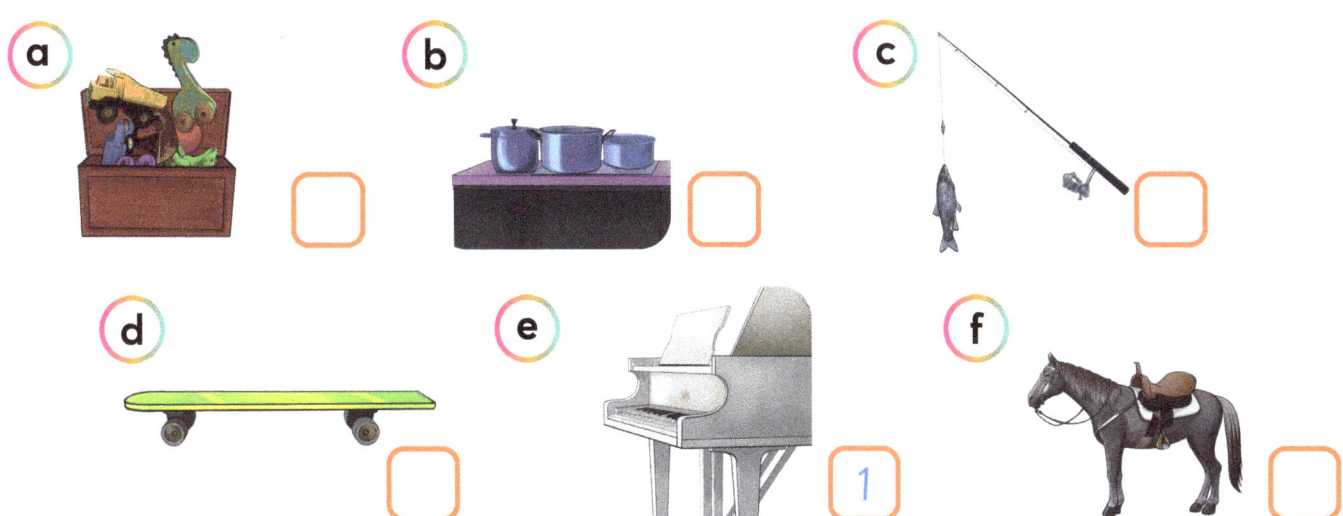

**2** Look 🔍 and match ✏️.

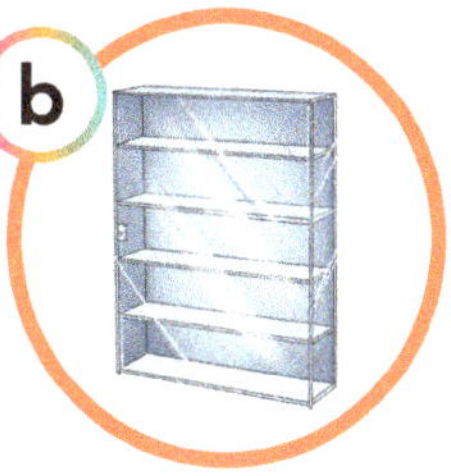

**Fast finishers** Make a list of the hobbies you know.

**How do you feel? Colour.**

# Nova Stars Unit 49 — Vocabulary

**1** Read and match. Say. | 5 |

- play the piano
- fish
- ride a horse
- collect
- go skateboarding
- cook

**2** Read and write. | 4 |

> play   ride   go   collect   ~~cook~~

1 I can ___cook___ dinner.
2 I can _____ lots of things.
3 I can _____ a horse.
4 I can _____ skateboarding with my friends.
5 I can _____ the piano.

**Fast finishers** Which hobby is missing from activity 2? Draw it.

How do you feel? Colour.

Nova Stars Unit 49 — Grammar

**1 Look and write .** 3

1. _I like_ riding a horse.

2. _____ fishing.

3. _____ cooking dinner.

4. _____ collecting things.

**2 Draw and write about your hobbies .** 4

1.

2.

I like _____ .          I don't like _____ .

**Fast finishers** Ask a friend *Which hobbies do you like?*

**How do you feel? Colour.**

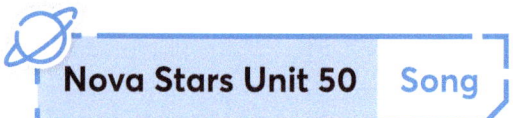 **Nova Stars Unit 50** Song

# We like playing sports

**1** Watch the music video 🎵 and tick ✓ the sports you see ✏️.

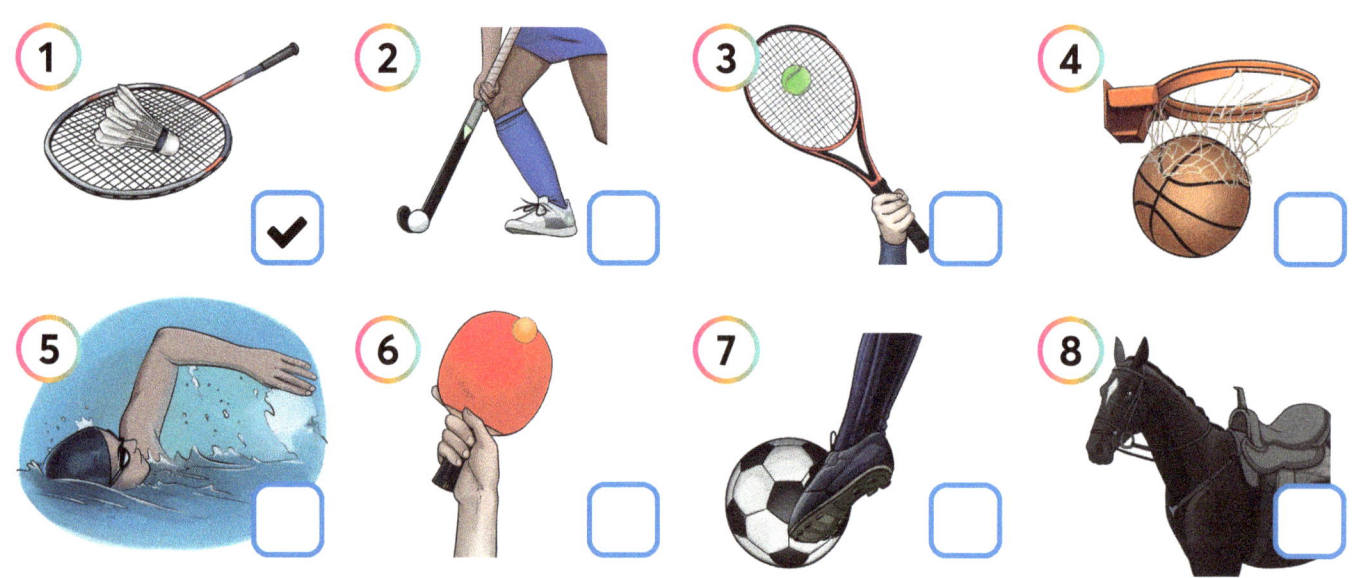

**2** Look 🔍 and match ✏️.

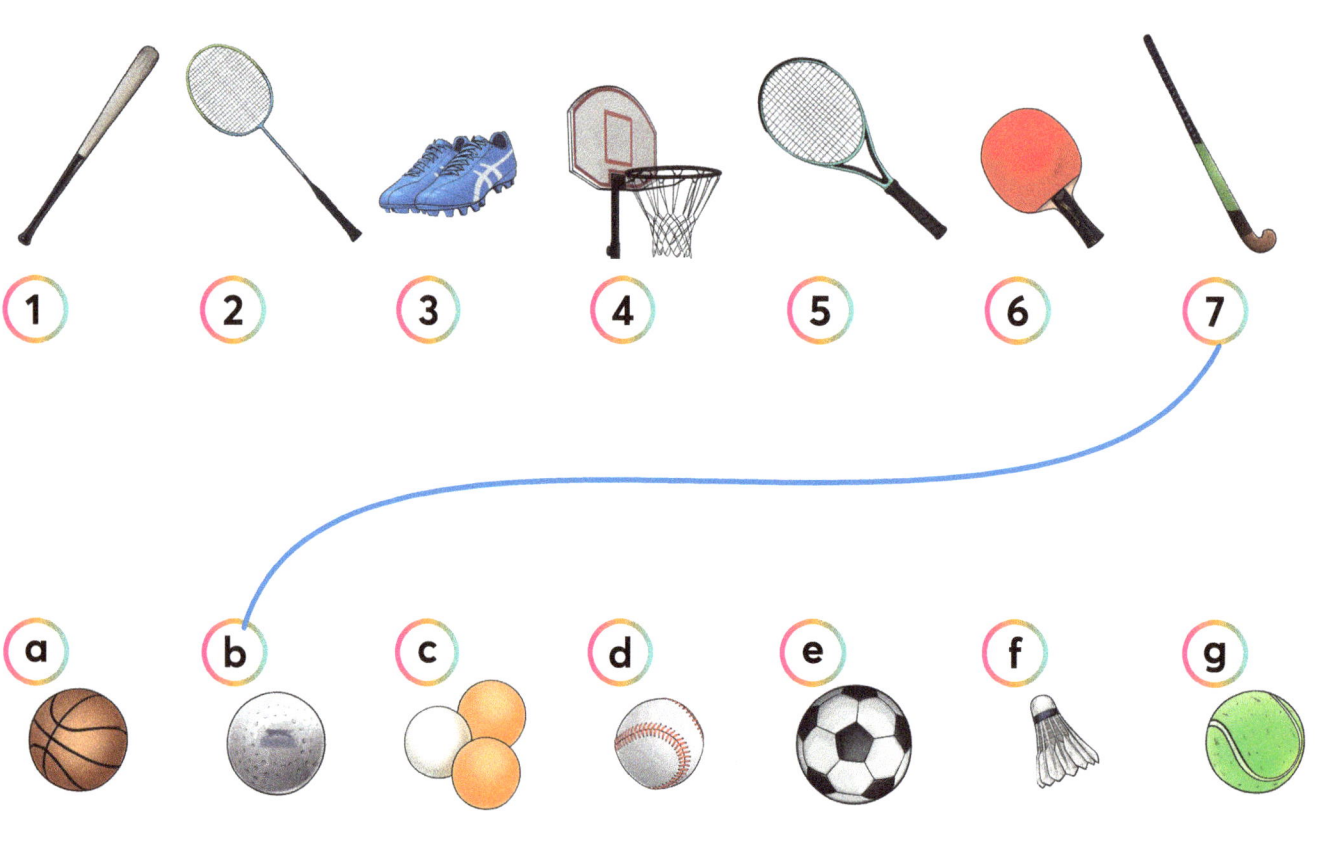

**Fast finishers** Draw and colour balls for three different sports.

**How do you feel? Colour.**

**Nova Stars Unit 50** — Vocabulary

**1** Read and circle. Say. | 5 |

1. tennis
   (hockey)

2. baseball
   basketball

3. tennis
   table tennis

4. badminton
   hockey

5. baseball
   table tennis

6. table tennis
   football

**2** Look and write. | 5 |

Sam     Ela

1  I like playing basketball. _Sam_

2  I don't like playing tennis. ⎯⎯⎯

3  I like playing football. ⎯⎯⎯

4  I don't like playing badminton. ⎯⎯⎯

5  I like playing table tennis. ⎯⎯⎯

6  I don't like playing baseball. ⎯⎯⎯

**Fast finishers** Which sports don't use a ball? Write a list.

**How do you feel? Colour.**

**Nova Stars Unit 50** Grammar

**1** Read, find  and write the letter . 5

1 We don't like playing football. _b_ and ........
2 I like playing basketball. ........
3 We like playing tennis. ........ and ........
4 I don't like playing table tennis. ........

**2** What do you and your friend like playing? Tick ✓ or cross ✗ and write . 4

like   don't like

 We ........................................................ .

 We ........................................................ .

 We ........................................................ .

 We ........................................................ .

 **Fast finishers** Write two more sentences about sports you and your friend like / don't like.

How do you feel? Colour.

# It's the weekend

Nova Stars Unit 51 Song

**1** Watch the music video 🎵 and match ✏️.

**2** Find 🔍 and colour the matching picture ✏️.

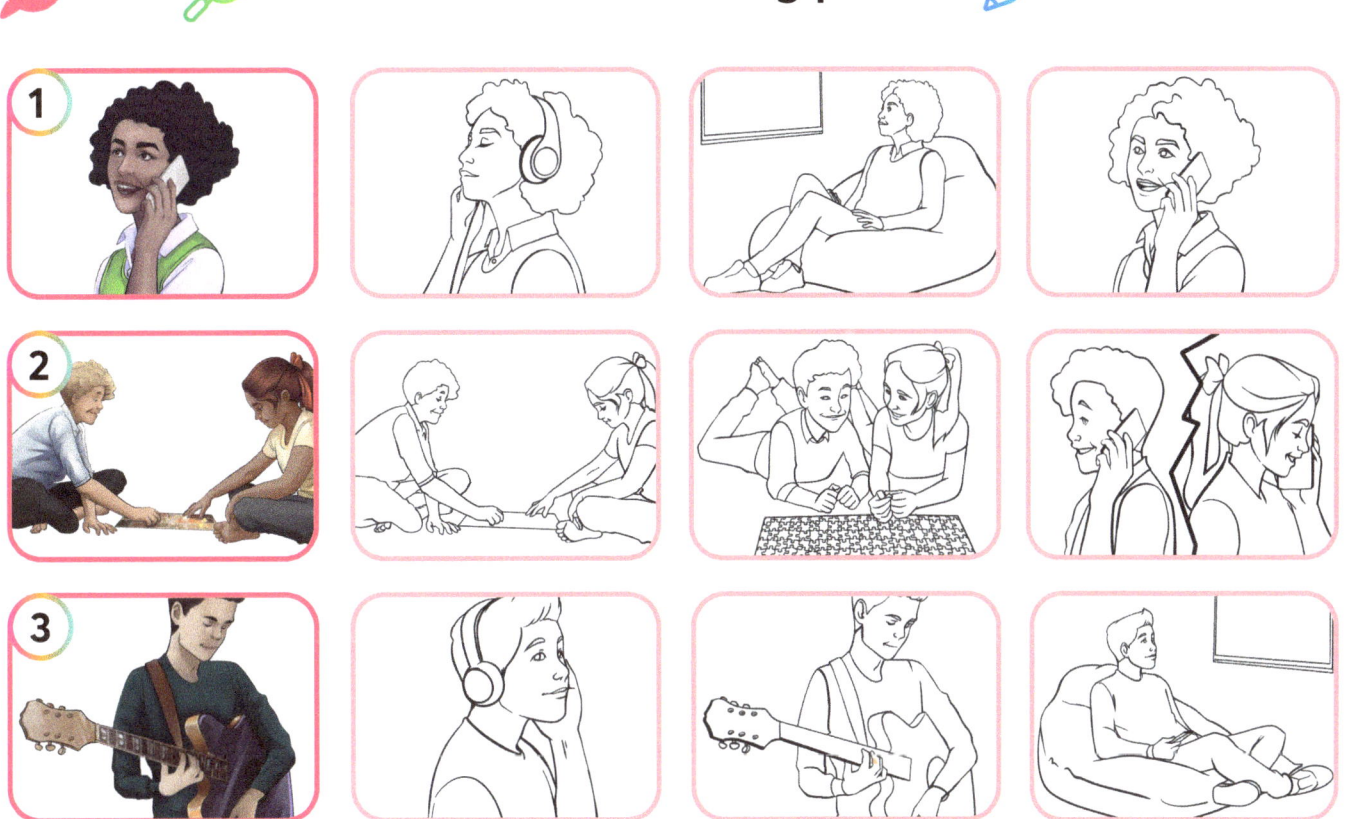

**Fast finishers** Circle and colour the activities you enjoy.

How do you feel? Colour.

**Nova Stars Unit 51** | **Vocabulary**

### 1 Read and circle. Say. | 5

do puzzles        listen to music        play a board game

talk on the phone        play the guitar        watch TV

### 2 Look, match and write. | 5

TV   puzzles   phone   music   guitar   ~~board game~~

play a ........ *board game* ........

do ................................

talk on the ................................

listen to ................................

play the ................................

watch ................................

**Fast finishers** What other things can you *play*? Tell your friend.

**How do you feel? Colour.**

## Nova Stars Unit 51 — Grammar

**1** Read, find and write the letter.

1 He isn't doing puzzles. He's talking on the phone. _d_
2 She isn't playing a board game. She's playing the guitar. ......
3 She isn't watching TV. She's listening to music. ......
4 He isn't playing the guitar. He's watching TV. ......

**2** What is David doing? Look and write.

1 He's _playing a board game_ and listening to ..................... .
2 He ..................... TV.
3 He ..................... doing puzzles or talking on the ..................... .
4 ..................... guitar.

**Fast finishers** Point at different people on this page. Say what he / she is doing.

**How do you feel? Colour.**

**Nova Stars Unit 52** Song

# Time to do your chores

**1** Watch the music video . Circle the activities you see .

**2** Look  and match .

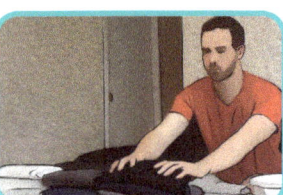   

**Fast finishers** Circle the activities you do at home.

**How do you feel? Colour.**

Nova Stars Unit 52 · Vocabulary

**1** Look, read and match. Say. ☐ 5

clean the windows — fold the clothes — tidy the living room

walk the dog — wash the car — water the plants

**2** Look at Activity 1 again. Read and write. ☐ 5

~~Alice~~   David   Hugo   Jack   May   DJ Nat

1 She isn't walking the dog. She's tidying the living room. *Alice*.
2 He isn't watering the plants. He's cleaning the windows. _____.
3 She isn't folding the clothes. She's watering the plants. _____.
4 He isn't washing the car. He's folding the clothes. _____.
5 She isn't cleaning the windows. She's walking the dog. _____.
6 He isn't tidying the living room. He's washing the car. _____.

**Fast finishers** Mime doing a chore. Your partner guesses: *You're …*

How do you feel? Colour.

**Nova Stars Unit 52** Grammar

**1** Look , read and write . 3

1  Is he washing the car?
No, he isn't.

2  Is she walking the dog?
_____

3  Is he watering the plants?
_____

4  Is she tidying the living room?
_____

**2** Draw a friend doing a chore. Then circle and write . 4

What's he / she doing?

Is he / she _____?

No, he / she isn't.

_____?

Yes, _____.

He's / She's _____!

**Fast finishers** Complete activity 2 again with a different friend.

How do you feel? Colour.

# What does she do everyday?

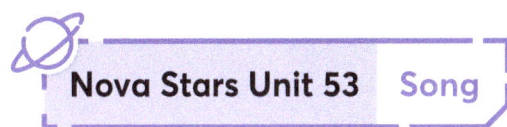 Nova Stars Unit 53 Song

**1** Watch the music video 🎵 and number ✏️.

**2** Look 🔍 and find the daily routine ✏️.

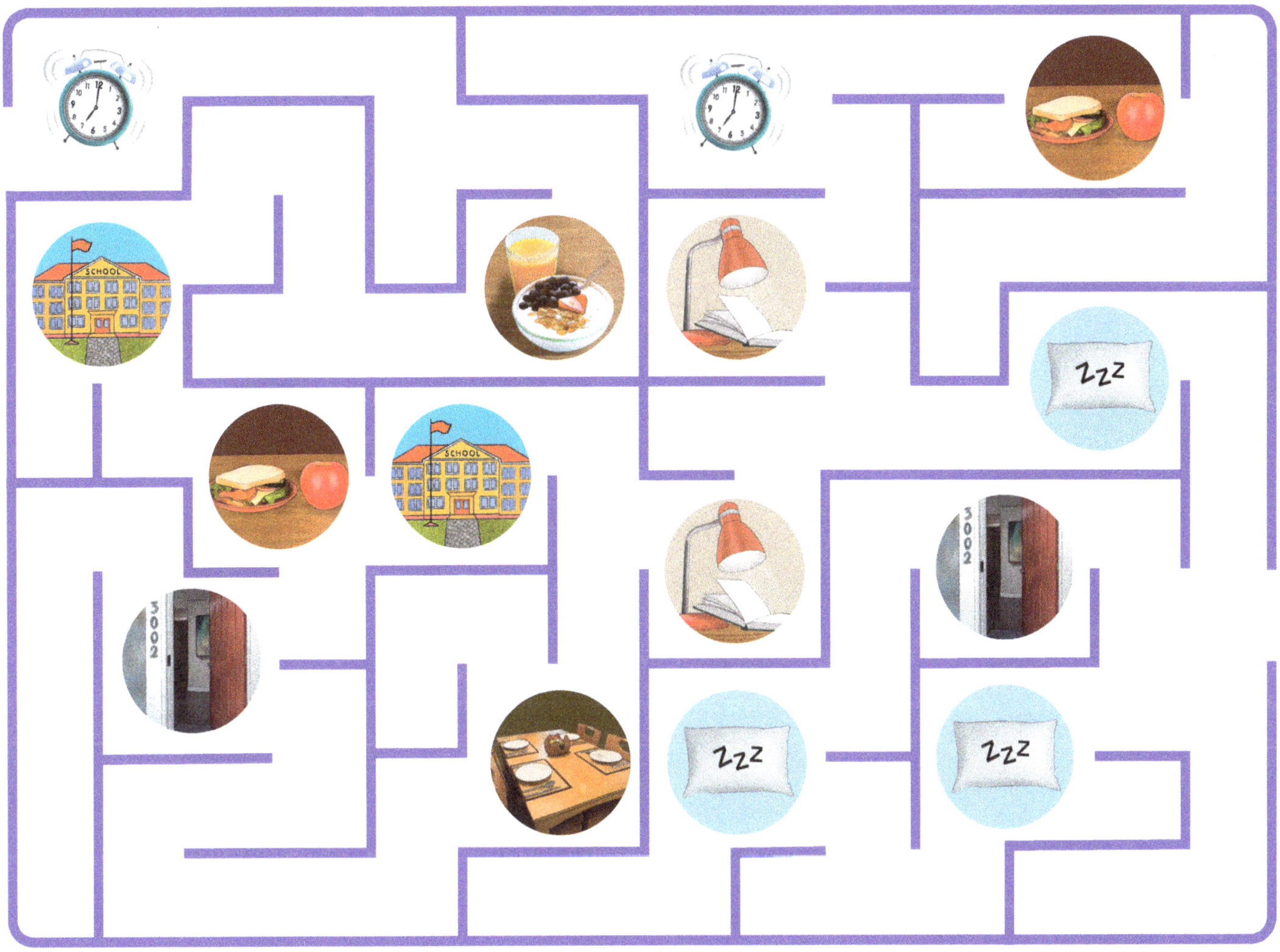

**Fast finishers** What's your favourite lunch? Draw and say.

**How do you feel? Colour.**

# Nova Stars Unit 53 — Vocabulary

**1** Find and circle 8 activities. Say. | 7 |

cle(getup)wongotosleepleavgotoschoolonthhavelunchtowfo
feehavebreakfastprogotoworknitgohomewavhavedinnerhe

**2** Look and write the words from activity 1. Which activity is missing? | 6 |

I _get up_ at 7 o'clock. Then I _____. I _____ on foot. I _____ with my friends. I _____ at 3 o'clock. I _____ with my family. At 9 o'clock, I _____.

**Fast finishers** Write sentences about your daily routine.

How do you feel? Colour.

**Nova Stars Unit 53** Grammar

**1** Look , read and circle .  5

1. DJ Nat **gets up** / **get up**.
She **have** / **has** breakfast.
Then she **goes** / **go** to work.

2. DJ Nat **go** / **goes** home.
She **has** / **have** dinner.
Then she **go** / **goes** to sleep.

**2** Look  and read . Tick ✔ or ✘ the sentences . 5

✘ May has lunch at home.

☐ DJ Dan goes to work.

☐ Ben goes home at 4 o'clock.

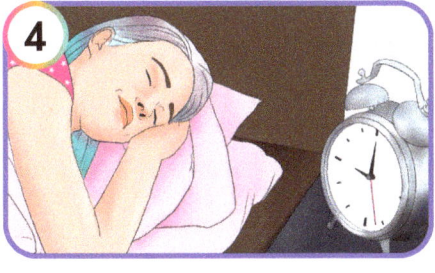

☐ Alice goes to sleep at 10 o'clock.

☐ Tom goes to work.

☐ Zuzu has dinner with her family.

**Fast finishers** Write 4 sentences about a friend's daily routine.

**How do you feel? Colour.**

**Nova Stars Unit 54** Song

# My dad's daily routine

**1** Watch the music video 🎵 and match ✏️.

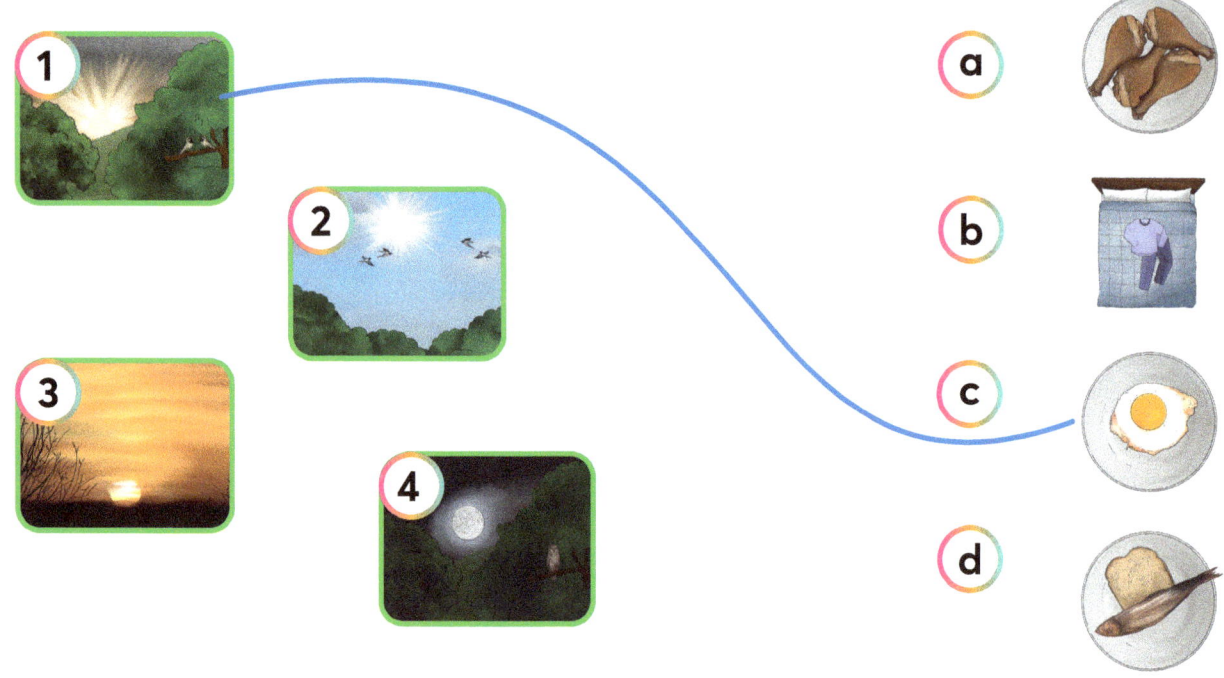

**2** Watch again. Look 🔍 and tick ✔ the photos for May's dad ✏️.

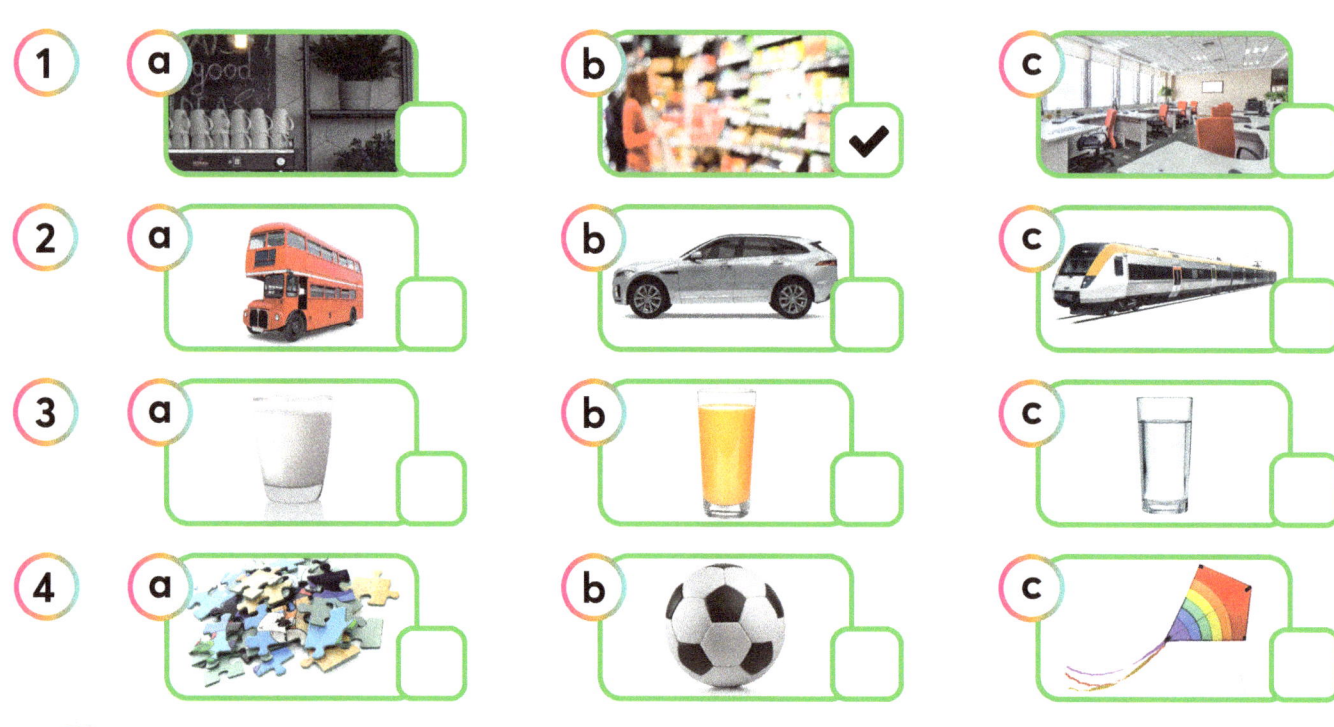

**Fast finishers** What do you have for breakfast, lunch and dinner? Write a list.

**How do you feel? Colour.**

# Nova Stars Unit 54 — Vocabulary

**1** Look and write. Say. [4]

in the morning    in the evening    in the afternoon    at night

**1**

**2**

**3**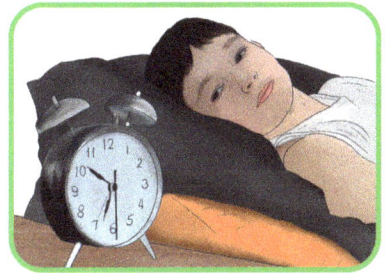

**4**

**2** Read and write. [3]

1 I have breakfast *in the morning*.
2 I have lunch ................................................................ .
3 I have dinner ............................................................... .
4 I go to bed .................................................................. .

**Fast finishers** Answer the questions: What time do you get up in the morning? What time do you have dinner in the evening? What time do you go to bed at night?

**How do you feel? Colour.**

# Nova Stars Unit 54 — Grammar

## 1 Look and tick ✓ the correct sentence. [3]

1.
   a He has breakfast at 7 o'clock.
   b He has breakfast at 8 o'clock. ✓
   c He has breakfast at 9 o'clock

2.
   a He drinks water in the evening.
   b He drinks milk in the evening.
   c He drinks juice in the evening.

3.
   a He eats fish for lunch.
   b He eats chicken for lunch.
   c He eats sausages in the afternoon.

4.
   a He goes to work at night.
   b He goes to work in the morning.
   c He goes to work in the evening.

## 2 Read and write. [5]

> drinks   eats   ~~has~~
> has   goes   works

1 Amira __has__ breakfast in the morning.
2 She ......... eggs for her breakfast.
3 She ......... lunch at one o'clock.
4 She ......... in an office.
5 She ......... milk in the evening.
6 She ......... to bed at 10 o'clock.

Amira

**Fast finishers** Write some sentences about a friend or someone in your family.

How do you feel? Colour.

# On the beach

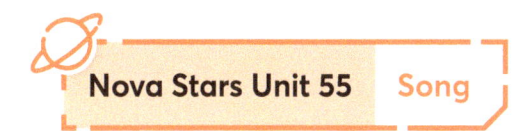 Nova Stars Unit 55 | Song

**1** Watch the music video 🎵 and number.

 a

 b

 c

 d 1

 e

**2** Find 🔍 and circle six differences ✏️.

 1

 2

**Fast finishers** Circle the activities on this page that you like.

**How do you feel? Colour.**

**Nova Stars Unit 55** — Vocabulary

**1** Look, read and match. Say. | 5

1 shell
2 ship
3 beach
4 sea
5 sand
6 jellyfish

a  b  c  d  e  f

**2** Read and write. | 5

1 Let's play in the <u>s a n d</u>.
2 Let's swim in the _ _ _ .
3 Look! A _ _ _ _ is sailing on the sea.
4 Be careful! That's a _ _ _ _ _ _ _ _ _ _ !
5 I like collecting _ _ _ _ _ _ _ .
6 Look at the sand on the _ _ _ _ _ _ .

**Fast finishers** Write three sentences with *Let's…* about the beach.

How do you feel? Colour.

**Nova Stars Unit 55** Grammar

**1** Read and write *Yes, please* or *No, thanks*. | 3

1. Would you like to play in the sand?
😊 Yes, please.

2. Would you like to see a jellyfish?
☹️ _____

3. Would you like to collect some shells?
☹️ _____

4. Would you like to swim in the sea?
😊 _____

**2** Read and write. | 4

1. play in the sand? → Would you like to play in the sand?

2. go to the beach? → _____

3. dance and sing? → _____

4. play football? → _____

5. go skateboarding? → _____

**Fast finishers** Answer the questions in activity 2.

**How do you feel? Colour.**

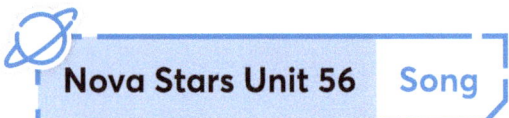

## The sea is nice and blue

**1** Watch the music video 🎵. Tick ✓ the things in the song ✏️.

**2** Look 🔍 and match ✏️.

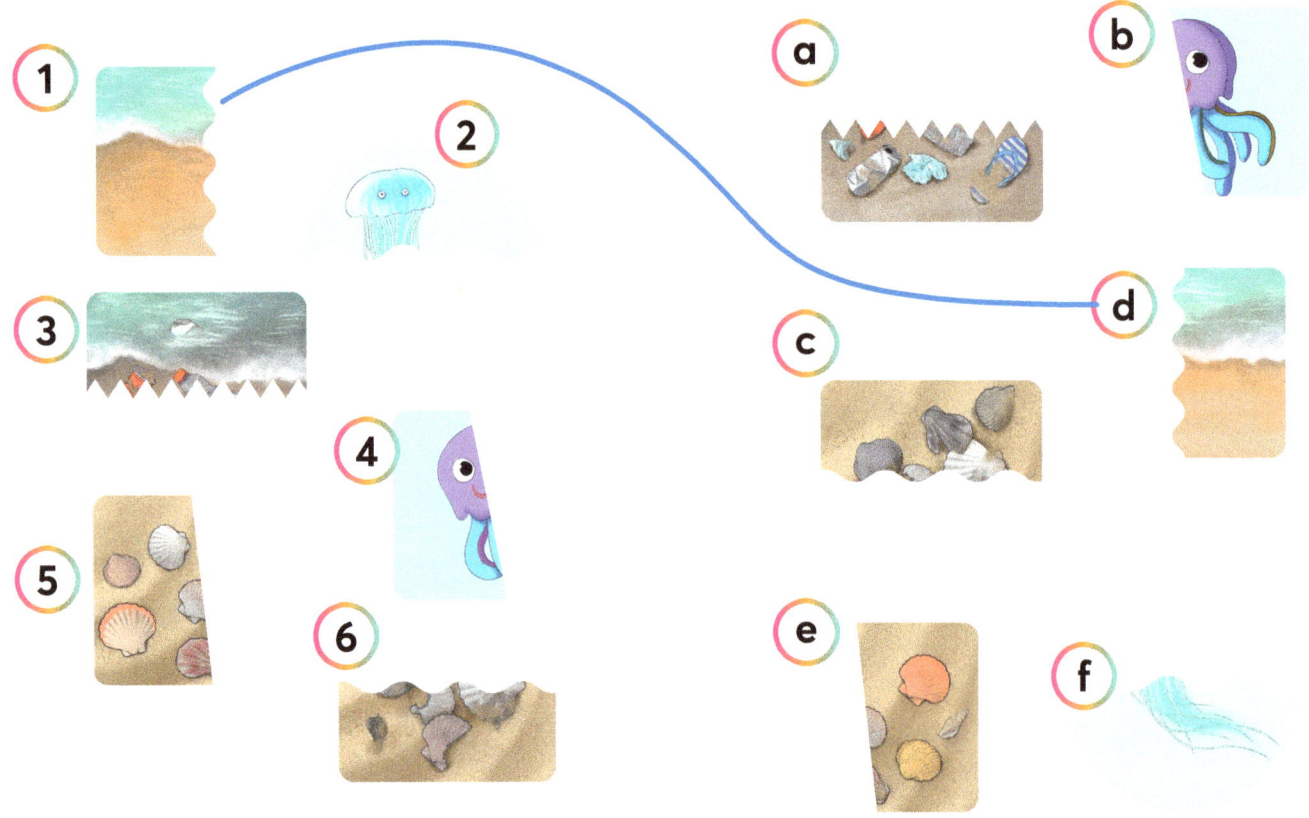

**Fast finishers** Can you remember the words in activity 2? Say.

How do you feel? Colour.

# Nova Stars Unit 56 | Vocabulary

**1** Read and match. Say. 5

beautiful   clean   dirty   fun   scary   ugly

**2** Look and write. 5

1 ___It's___ ugly.    2 They're c_____.

3 _____ s_____.    4 _____ b_____.

5 _____ f_____.    6 _____ d_____.

**Fast finishers** How many shells are there in activity 1? Count and write a sentence with *There* …

**How do you feel? Colour.**

# Nova Stars Unit 56 Grammar

**1** Look, read and circle. | 3 |

1. (This)/ That beach is clean.

2. Those / These jellyfish are fun.

3. This / That ship is ugly.

4. Those / These shells are beautiful.

**2** Look and write sentences with *This, That, These* or *Those*. | 3 |

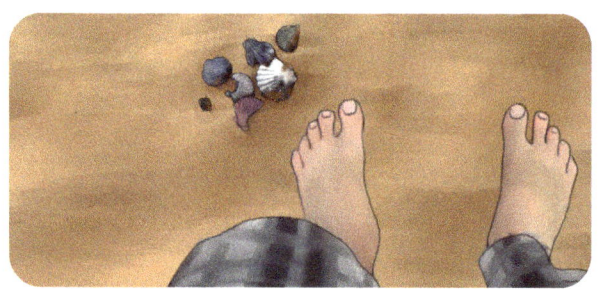
1  Those shells are ugly.

2 _____ is dirty.

3 _____ clean.   4 _____

**Fast finishers** Write two sentences with *This … That … These …* or *Those …*

**How do you feel? Colour.**

# On my street

**Nova Stars Unit 57 Song**

**1** Watch the music video 🎵 and match ✏️.

  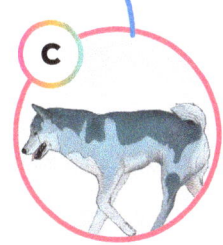  

**2** Find 🔍 and circle 6 differences ✏️.

**Fast finishers** Write a list of 5 activities you can see in the pictures.

**How do you feel? Colour.**

# Nova Stars Unit 57 — Vocabulary

**1** Look, follow and circle. Say. [7]

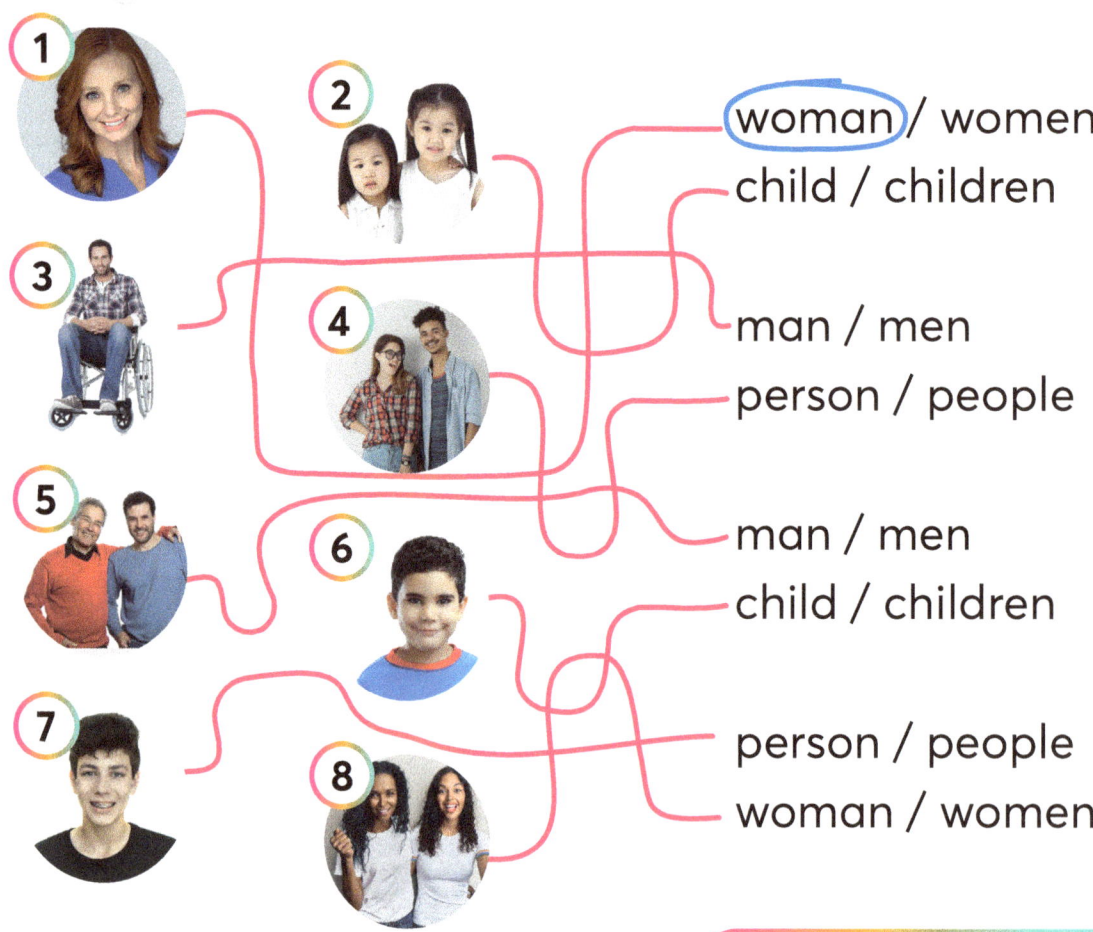

- (woman) / women
- child / children
- man / men
- person / people
- man / men
- child / children
- person / people
- woman / women

**2** Look and write. [5]

| man | person | women |
| ~~men~~ | woman | people |

1. men
2. 
3. 
4. 
5. 
6. 

**Fast finishers** Draw three children in the park.

**How do you feel? Colour.**

## 1 Read and tick. 3

**1** She isn't reading a book.

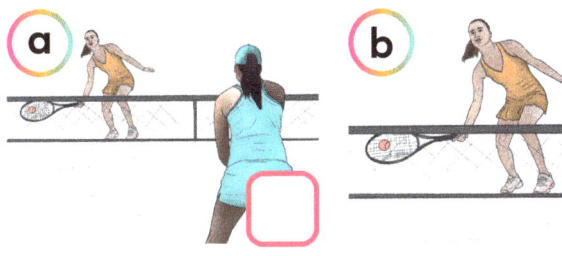

**2** They're drinking water.

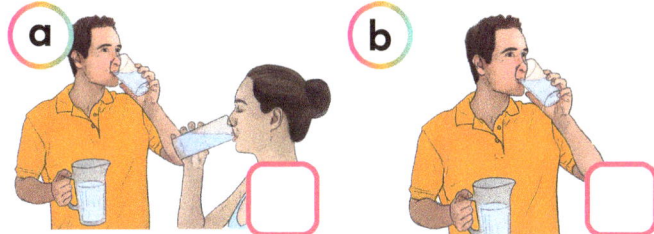

**3** They're eating ice creams.

**4** They aren't playing football.

## 2 Look and write. 3

drinking water   ~~doing a puzzle~~   listening to music
reading a book   singing

What are Lily and David doing?

They're  doing a puzzle.

They aren't ................................................

................................................

They ................................................

and ................................................

**Fast finishers** Write two more sentences about what Lily and David aren't doing.

**How do you feel? Colour.**

**Nova Stars Unit 58** Song

# They are sitting in the sun

**1** Watch the music video and number.

a  b  c  d  e  f

☐  1  ☐  ☐  ☐  ☐

**2** Look. Read and tick.

1  Is Alex playing football?      Yes, he is. ☐   No, he isn't. ✓
2  Is Grace swimming?              Yes, she is. ☐  No, she isn't. ☐
3  Is David playing the guitar?    Yes, he is. ☐   No, he isn't. ☐
4  Is Sarah walking?               Yes, she is. ☐  No, she isn't. ☐
5  Is Zoe watching TV?             Yes, she is. ☐  No, she isn't. ☐
6  Is Grace having lunch?          Yes, she is. ☐  No, she isn't. ☐

**Fast finishers** What is Zoe doing in activity 2? What is David doing? Write two sentences.

**How do you feel? Colour.**

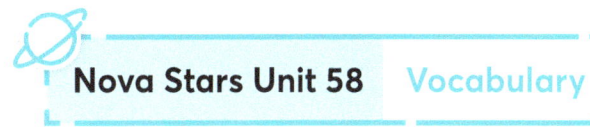

**Nova Stars Unit 58** Vocabulary

### 1. Read and match. Say. | 5 |

sit in the sun    have an ice cream

drive    skip    wave    take photos

### 2. Look and write. | 5 |

driving    skipping    ~~waving~~    taking photos
sitting in the sun    having an ice cream

1.  He is _waving._

2.  She is _____

3.  She is _____

4.  He is _____

5.  She is _____

6.  He is _____

 **Fast finishers** What can you do? Write two sentences with *I can / can't…*

**How do you feel? Colour.**

# Nova Stars Unit 58 — Grammar

**1** Look and write questions. Answer the questions.

Yes, they are    No, they aren't

1 Find Alice and Hugo — they / sit in the sun?
  Are they sitting in the sun?   Yes, they are.

2 Find Jack and Lily — they / have an ice cream?

3 Find Tom and Ben — they / drive?

4 Find Jack and Kim — they / wave?

5 Find Alice and Grace — they / take photos?

6 Find Grace, Lily and Ben — they / play with a ball?

**Fast finishers** With a friend, ask and answer *Are they …ing?* questions about other people in your classroom.

How do you feel? Colour.

Printed in the USA
CPSIA information can be obtained
at www.ICGtesting.com
CBHW061055200724
11806CB00053B/748